evangelism men:
Preaching for Decision

James A. Ponder
Compiler

BROADMAN PRESS
Nashville, Tennessee

4262-25
ISBN: 0-8054-6225

Dewey Decimal Classification: 269.2
Subject heading: EVANGELISTIC SERMONS
Library of Congress Catalog Card Number: 75-55685
Printed in the United States of America

Contents

Foreword

James A. Ponder, secretary of evangelism for the Florida Baptist Convention, has compiled a book of sermons entitled, *Evangelism Men: Preaching for Decision*. The compiler's own heart beats for evangelism. He has selected what he calls "evangelistic preaching at its finest." The contents are grounded upon the Word of God, bathed in compassionate prayer, and directed toward life-changing decisions.

James Ponder has chosen some of the finest evangelists and men of God in compiling this book. These men represent a body of faithful, called-out, gifted men as vocational evangelists. They are all personal witnesses and convincing preachers.

The primary purpose of evangelistic preaching is to call men to a personal commitment by repentance and faith to Jesus Christ as Savior and Lord. These messages blend sound theology and practical experience with a clear, convincing call for decision. "For whosoever shall call upon the name of the Lord shall be saved" (Rom. 10:13). "As many as received him, to them gave he power to become the sons of God, even to them that believe on his name" (John 1:12).

These evangelists have preached for decision in churches and crusades across America. Their messages were not prepared for them for publication, but are their fervent messages proclaiming the gospel with the desire to reach the lost, and preaching for decision.

—BILLY GRAHAM
Montreat, North Carolina

Introduction

God has gifted some to be evangelists as he has some to be pastors and other teachers. Each fit the fabric and pattern of God's plan for Christian proclamation.

Historically these proclaimers have been used in mighty manifestations when revival came both to churches and communities. Some were used in church building, spiritual growth for the fellowship, and membership enlargement. Others became area-wide preachers touching many churches, causing whole communities to turn toward God with significant moral stability and Christian witness. Their contribution to the task and joy of winning persons to Christ may have been underestimated on earth by some but are worth the record of heaven.

The contributors to this volume are men of such evangelism tradition. Each is distinctly gifted and each makes a decided impact through their specific ministry. Their messages are biblically sound and reflect compassionate zeal. Their experience reflects wide success through commitment to the call of their task. They are my friends. I commend them as the Master's choice evangelists.

C. B. HOGUE
Director, Evangelism Section
Baptist Home Mission Board

1

The Suicide of a Soul

Jack R. Taylor

And as He was setting out on a journey, a man ran up to Him and knelt before Him, and began asking Him, "Good Teacher, what shall I do to inherit eternal life?" And Jesus said to him, "Why do you call Me good? No one is good except God alone. You know the commandments, 'Do not murder, Do not commit adultery, Do not steal, Do not bear false witness, Do not defraud, Honor your Father and Mother.'" And he said to Him, "Teacher, I have kept all these things from my youth up." And looking at him, Jesus felt a love for him, and said to him, "One thing you lack: go and sell all you possess, and give it to the poor, and you shall have treasure in heaven; and come, and follow me." But at these words his face fell, and he went away grieved, for he was one who owned much property. MARK 10:17-22, NASB

There is something peculiarly shocking about a suicide. A brutal murder arouses our indignation, and we clamor for the arrest and punishment of the criminal. Pity is struck dumb by the sight of the shedding of innocent blood, and we forget to be merciful when justice draws her sword. But in the case of a suicide, the victim and the criminal are one and the same person. The one who committed the crime is dead, having died by his own hand. There is something untouchable about the regret that accompanies suicide. Just this day I talked with a father and mother whose son chose this means as a sudden exit out of his problems. There is not much one can say. We cannot but pity the wretchedness that prompted it, the haunting depression, the fears, the misery. Life must indeed seem horrible when, to escape it, one will deliberately leap into an open grave, a victim of his own hand.

It is a terrible thing to kill the body, to plunge into the tomb while the sun is shining and the birds are singing and the flowers are blooming. It is infinitely worse to destroy the soul, to deliberately take the path that leads to darkness and despair and to see the door of hope forever shut against us.

In the narrative of the rich young ruler we are given the picture of a spiritual suicide. It is perhaps the saddest, most haunting story in the New Testament. We are prone to remark, "If only . . . if only . . ." But a few remarks and the story is over and the die is cast . . . the decision made!

How rich were the possibilities. Here was a young man; a prominent young man; a religious, prominent, young man. He had surely heard of the Galilean prophet, and there had dawned upon him the infinite possibility of life eternal. He had decided, quite upon his own initiative, to come and see for himself and ask for himself life's most important question, "What shall I do that I might inherit eternal life?" At that throbbing moment, as he asked the question, the stage was set for the greatest of life's miracles. He was on the verge of a new life, eternal life, life from above, life in its highest state. I want you to notice four things that speak of the ideal nature of the moment:

1. He came at the right time. He was young and he stood to save a life as well as a soul. He might have heard the exhortation of Solomon of old as he said, "Remember now thy Creator in the days of thy youth . . ." (Eccl. 12:1).

2. He came in the right spirit. He came running and kneeling. Though a ruler, he came in the spirit of unveiled urgency and unapologetic humility.

3. He came for the right thing. Even his question was right. The commodity he sought was correct. He had plenty

of this world's goods but he knew he needed something else, eternal life!

4. He came to the right place and person. He came to Jesus. It is interesting that when the world has spoken its last hope and that hope has died ... folks head for Jesus. He is the only one who knows of eternal life.

I am not at all surprised that Jesus loved him. What a fine, splendid young man he must have been. We would have been glad to have him in our church, in our deacon group, on our finance committee, with our visitation team. Jesus loved him, but Jesus lost him because when he made the proposition, the young man looked at the price he must pay and turned away sorrowful. This simply supports the fact that a soul may be lost whom Jesus loves and that something more than the love of the Savior is essential for that soul to be saved!

"And he went away!" No sadder words have ever been written. And as he went away, Jesus watched him go and let him go! He did not lower the qualifications, compromise, or name a lesser price. He let him go! Jesus demanded a price the rich young ruler refused to pay.

My friend, Jesus today will demand the same of you. In all the years since that dramatic confrontation Jesus has not lowered his demands. If you come to him be assured that he will demand total commitment. It is lordship or nothing! I have the conviction that if Jesus was going to lower the qualifications for anyone, it would have been that splendid young man for whom he felt great love. And if Jesus was ever to take anyone on any less demands, he would have to apologize to the rich young ruler and cancel his eternal punishment.

Right beside this story in the Gospel of Luke there is the story of blind Bartimaeus. This poor man threw away his cloak, the only thing he had of any value, and came to Jesus just for the privilege of looking at the flowers and the stars and the sea, and immediately received his sight and followed Jesus. Do you think he mourned the loss of a cloak when he saw the face of the Savior!

The sad thing about this story is that it is not old. It is occurring every day. It may occur as you read this message. You may go away and not know until later, too late that there was in your life a soul's suicide. It is well, then, that we examine this story well. Take a good look at this young man. May God help you to make a wiser decision.

I want us to observe three things: First, I want you to observe what he had. Satisfaction is the one thing we are all looking for, but it is something we will never find except in Jesus Christ. To hunger no more, neither thirst is God's picture of those who unconditionally give themselves to Jesus, but no one has ever found that satisfaction anywhere else in the world.

The young man had wealth, but it did not satisfy him. Many of us can remember the time when we honestly felt that an unlimited bank account would guarantee contentment. But we have found that our destiny does not end here and that death presents its calling card as readily to the rich as to the poor. Golden locks cannot bar its approach. Gold can purchase many things in this world's markets but it is not current in the kingdom of God. In Lowell's "The Vision of Sir Launfal" we read:

> At the devil's booth all things are sold,
> Each ounce of dross costs an ounce of gold;
> For a cap and bells our lives we pay,
> Bubbles we buy with a whole soul's tasking;
> 'Tis heaven alone that is given away,
> 'Tis only God may be had for the asking.

Pleasure is what we all want, but we fail to secure it because we go to the wrong place seeking it. Silk covers as much brokenheartedness as calico. Your investment portfolio may impress your investment counselor but not the judge of your soul. You will never have satisfaction without Jesus!

The young man had social rank but his heart was hungry. We seem today to be preoccupied with the thought that if we can only know someone of social stature and mingle among those of the higher strata our hearts would find rest. But rest is not to be found in the social stratosphere any more than in the social dungeons of the world. The human heart hungers for something sweeter than the flatteries of this world, for a garment more beautiful than the product of a worm, and a jewel more precious than that found in the oyster. It is only when we stand before the king, and wear the robe that he provides, and hear from him his "well done," that the human heart enters into perfect contentment.

The rich young ruler had religion, but no peace of soul. He was a member of the orthodox church and lived up to its external requirements. He could look the Ten Commandments in the face without a blush. There was no skeleton in the closet of his memory. From his youth he had walked in the path of virtue, and yet, down deep in his soul there was a hunger for something he did not have. He knew he lacked something for there was in the midst of plenty on one hand a certain emptiness and craving that spoke of the existence of something more. And alas, it takes more than external religion to save a man from hell. The fact that he had lived within the approval of the Commandments without breaking them is nothing to God. A statue chiseled out of stone breaks none of them either, but that fact does not make the piece of stone a saint. It will not make you a saint either, my friend.

With all that he had, he really had nothing that mattered for eternity. He had nothing that he could not lose. When he went to bed at night he did not know but that with the coming of morning all that he had would be gone.

This reminds me of a locomotive used in a great railway system of a prior day. It looks perfect but it takes twenty men a half hour to move it thirty feet. No bolt, no bar, no wheel was missing, and yet the great machine designed to pull great trains at sixty miles an hour could not even move itself. The problem? It lacked fire in the furnace, water in the boiler, steam in the tubes. The young man of our text lacked the indwelling power of the Holy Spirit.

I am not condemning your wealth or social position. They are splendid in their places, but they are not substitutes for the grace of God that brings salvation. They simply will not do when we are dying!

We have observed what he had, now let us observe, secondly, what he was offered. I am not sure what this young man expected to hear as an answer to his question. I have never quite agreed with those who suggest that he came to display his moral excellence. His running, kneeling, and crying seem to seal the matter of his sincerity to me. But even the fact of his sincerity did not serve to save his soul.

He was offered a Savior. If you miss this, you will miss it all. What you need is Jesus, himself, not another philosophy to complete life, not another addendum to all that you already have. You need Jesus, nothing more, nothing less. It would be easier if life could be sealed with a set of doctrines or the joining of an organization, but it does not come that way. What Jesus was saying was precisely the same as he had said to Nicodemus, "Ye must be born again" (John 3:7). This experience is not giving consent to a new creed, but the total rebirth of the person. It is the soul receiving an inheritance without being paid an immediate wage, and if we are not careful, we are apt to judge the cost too great and the reward too little. This caused a fatal decision on the part of the rich young ruler. But the seeming loss is only in appearance. It is the loss of the acorn for the oak tree, the loss of the flower for the fruit, the loss of our life for the gaining of his life. Jesus did not discuss doctrines with this young man, but he offered himself as the solution to all his problems. Salvation, then, is not the assent to a set of doctrines but the reception of Jesus himself into the life. It is still true that "as many as received him, to them gave he power to become the sons of God" (John 1:12).

Jesus offered this young man a cross. Whatever our age does to dress up the cross and make it a beautiful ornament, it still stands for death, the termination of life. It stands for the beginning of one way of life and the end of another. What Jesus was offering this young man was a life of identification with the needs of others, a life of redemption, a life you can never have while putting yourself first. The cross in our lives means that we have died to former plans, concerns, and affections to be made alive to all that God has planned in Jesus Christ in us.

The young man was not asked to throw away his wealth, but to make it redemptive in the lives of others. Jesus knew that until this young man was willing to become truly redemptive he would never really follow Jesus at all.

The young man was offered a destiny. "Thou shalt find treasure in heaven ..." (Matt. 19:21). Who understands the depth and width of this promise? Wise investors are bound to always take the long look. They will give up a thing of value to achieve out across the years a thing of far greater value. So in coming to Christ and following him there is the deep satisfaction that though we cannot take our riches with us we can certainly send them on ahead.

This was the supreme offer that the Savior made that

splendid young man that day. But he missed the point. In a moment, the big moment was gone never to return. That same offer is being made today—a Savior, a cross, a destiny—that same decision is being pondered. At stake is more than a life and a few years. There in the balances is a soul and eternity!

We have observed what he had and what he was offered, but let us now observe what he lacked. It is interesting that with all he had, his story is that of a colossal failure. With wealth, social standing, and religion, he is a classic failure. He missed it all on a seeming technicality. But, really, what was the issue? What did he lack?

He lacked a true conception of what real religion was. He may have believed he might get eternal life by some rite or ritual he had missed somewhere in his life. Perhaps he could obtain it by inheritance as he had much of what he did have. Here was a rich prodigal, a prodigal because he failed to let the Father have the right of way in his life. There are many hungry prodigals who never feed swine, for we are all prodigals until we yield Jesus right of way in our souls.

He lacked a surrendered will. I cannot help but think that in this one point is the issue of the whole story. Why did he really go away and was thus eternally lost as far as we have knowledge? Simply because he refused to bow his will to that of Jesus. He refused the lordship of Christ in his life. Where have we gotten away from the teaching of lordship as a requisite for salvation? You simply cannot accept Jesus as Savior alone without taking him as Lord. You may be saved without knowing much of his lordship, but you will never be saved refusing his lordship. Most of our soul-winning approaches have one haunting point of negligence, that of lordship. Let me say it clearly again: It is impossible to be saved without receiving Jesus the Lord! Any sinner who would turn back with the knowledge of the full and complete claims of Jesus as Lord of his life *should* turn back, for he can never come into the kingdom on any other basis than this. Jesus knew that there was a god in that young man's life that must be put to death. That god was money! He could never reign over the domain where money was Lord!

The test that Jesus put to this young man was that of the willingness to surrender his will. The revelation came that the young man wanted salvation, but he wanted it on his own terms. He wanted peace without surrender and to such a peace Jehovah will never capitulate. To have peace with God, he must recognize him as Victor!

The testing point may be somewhere else with you. It came at the point of wealth for the rich young ruler because that was the thing he supremely loved. He would give Jesus any place in his heart except that room in which his treasure was stored. He may ask of you and me the surrender of something else. Whatever we prize most highly he demands that we surrender it to him.

Finally, he lacked eternal life. He went away sorrowful. It was not a flippant decision made with a slight smile or jeer. He was not unkind and did not go away in a rage. He was sad because he knew that he was missing much. He had no idea just how much he was missing. The tragedy is that he went away. For all practical purposes he might as well have gone away in a rage or in shallow and mocking laughter. He made a choice for himself and found out too late that it was really against himself. He was both the victim and the criminal. He had *done* himself to death, and it was all over in a minute. The deed was done. "He went away." The curtain closes. "The End" is written on the story never, to our knowledge, to be reopened. That fine young man is in outer darkness today with no hope of repair. His state is terminal, eternal, hopeless. And to think that it all rode on the result of that one moment, when he considered for a long moment the proposition of the Savior and then walked away. What might have been still haunts us today as expressed by John Greenleaf Whittier:

> Of all sad words of tongue or pen,
> The saddest are, "it might have been."

Surely we can imagine that from the pits of hell there comes this hopeless cry:

> I plead today from Hell's cruel fire
>   And tell you now my last desire.
> You cannot do a thing for me . . .
>   No words today, my bonds will free.
>
> But do not err, my friend, again;
>   Do all you can for the souls of men.
> Plead with them now quite earnestly,
>   Lest they be cast in Hell with me.
>   JAMES RUSSELL LOWELL

Thus we see the profile of a spiritual suicide, the suicide of a soul.

I wonder if I am speaking today to some soul pondering life's greatest decision; someone who earnestly desires to enter into life eternal. You have tried what this world offers and have found it empty. You have come to discover that the cost to follow Christ is high. It will cost you everything you have, but do not forget you will receive all that he has and is. Let me plead with you to register a wiser decision than the rich young ruler. Let Jesus have his way with you, and there will come into your heart a sense of satisfaction.

Who is there who will lay aside all and follow him? Will you take him with the knowledge he demands of you, your will surrendered to him? And do you come knowing that he expects to be the commander-in-chief of your life from this moment on? Will you allow him to reign without a rival in

your life, beginning this very moment? All that you have
ever dreamed that you could be, all that you have ever
longed for, and more, will be yours here and hereafter in
Jesus and in him alone.

> Come, ye sinners, poor and needy,
> Weak and wounded, sick and sore;
> Jesus ready stands to save you,
> Full of pity, love, and pow'r.
>
> . . . .
>
> Come, ye weary, heavy-laden,
> Lost and ruined by the fall;
> If you tarry till you're better,
> You will never come at all.
>
> JOSEPH HART

Then say to him today:

> Just as I am, poor, wretched, blind;
> Sight, riches, healing of the mind,
> Yea, all I need in thee to find,
> O Lamb of God, I come! I come!
>
> CHARLOTTE ELLIOTT

2

Does Jesus Know You?

James Robison

Enter ye in at the strait gate: for wide is the gate, and broad is the way, that leadeth to destruction, and many there be which go in thereat: Because strait is the gate, and narrow is the way, which leadeth unto life, and few there be that find it.
MATTHEW 7:13-14

There are some people who don't believe in hell and would have to argue with Jesus about this particular verse. Jesus is all knowing. He is the essence of wisdom, knowledge, and all truth. He is truth. He says, "I am the truth" (John 14:6). Jesus says that there is a broad road that leads "to destruction, and many there be which go in thereat: Because strait is the gate, and narrow is the way, which leadeth unto life, and few there be that find it" (Matt. 7:13-14).

This contradicts most human philosophy. Most of us would like to think the majority of our world is on the road to hell. I heard a preacher say that we can win the world to Christ. I don't agree, because it won't hold water spiritually. The Bible teaches that we can teach and witness to the world, but the Bible also teaches that the majority of the world will never be saved. The way to life is strait and narrow. Few will find it.

It is the greatest discovery you will ever make when you discover the way of life. When you find it, you will discover it is not a plan, but it is a man. It is a person. It is not something you do, but someone you know. This someone is

20

Jesus Christ. Salvation is neither an ethic nor a principle. It is not a series of do's and don'ts. It is literally a spiritual rebirth, a new birth.

We hear a lot of talk today about being born again. Many people who talk about it know nothing about it. The born-again life brings about a spiritual transformation that literally causes an individual to become an adopted son or daughter of God. You become God's child. I don't know how many of you have ever come to know this life, but according to the Scriptures there are few who have. I don't want to be critical, but if the truth were known, many of you have never come to know this way of life.

Many know a religious way of life. There are many cheap substitutes for the way of life. Satan is quick to offer you a substitute. I can assure you that although religion is popular today, it is as useless as it has ever been in history. We have today in modern times "a bread and fish" religion. "Bread and fish religion" is demonstrated by folks running around looking for something that will make them feel better, fuller, and happier, just as the people who followed Jesus and saw him as a potential Messiah. They wanted him to become an earthly king and solve all their needs, illnesses, wants, famine, and poverty. Jesus said he wanted them to seek the meat that endures to eternal life. The people were running after more and more miracles.

We have a religion today that tells you that God is a cheap remedy to all that ails you. He is a big, glorified Band-Aid, apply where needed. He never meets your needs until you come to know him as the living, sovereign, mighty God that he really is. He is no cheap remedy to your aches and pains. He is not a bottle of medicine or an instrument we use for our own personal edification. He is God! Until you know him as God, you don't know him. He can fill your life with meaning and direction. He is the answer to every need.

When he thought of men's hungering hearts, he said, "I am the bread of life." When he thought of their souls, he said, "I am the water of life." When he thought of them groping in darkness, he said, "I am the light of the world." When he thought of their need for shelter, he said, "I am the door." When he thought of their desire for knowledge, he said, "I am the truth." When he thought of man's desire to live, he said, "I am the life." He said, "For whosoever will save his life shall lose it: and whosoever will lose his life for my sake shall find it. For what is a man profited, if he shall gain the whole world, and lose his own soul?" (Matt. 16:25). How many of you ever lost your life for Jesus' sake? I didn't say for the church's sake or for religion's sake, but for Jesus' sake. There is a difference.

Jesus is a personal Savior, and you must know him personally. There are so many who don't know his voice. They don't know him. Paul said, "Be no more children, tossed to and fro" (Eph. 4:14). They are unstable. They are double-minded. They are blown about by "every wind of doctrine" (v. 14). They don't know the truth when they hear it. They may be caught up in religious circles, but they don't know the truth. When the truth is in you, when you know Jesus, then you can distinguish the sounds. You know the truth. People flock to the truth, if they know the truth. They recognize it. They follow it. Jesus said, "My sheep hear my voice, and I know them, and they follow me" (John 10:27). The whole thing boils down to whether or not you know and follow Jesus. I hope you know him. You know whether or not you do.

Some of you say, "I'm a Baptist, myself." Isn't that wonderful! Some of the meanest people I have ever met are Baptists. I promise you, some of the biggest crooks in the United States of America are Baptists. Some of them may even be Baptist preachers. Some are evangelists. Some of the most royal rip-offs in the country are evangelist preachers. Are you a Baptist? One of our recent surveys in Texas showed that 72 percent of the inmates in Huntsville Penitentiary are Baptists. Some say, "I'm a Catholic." That doesn't make you a Christian. Being a Baptist doesn't make you a Christian either. Jesus makes you a Christian.

A Baptist boy in one of our crusades got concerned about one of his friends and he turned to him and said, "Would you like to be a Christian?" The boy turned to him and said, "I'm a Methodist." The Baptist boy asked, "Why are you a Methodist?" He replied, "My mother and daddy were Methodist, and my grandmother and grandfather were Methodist. I come from a long line of Methodists, so I'm a Methodist." The smart younster looked at him and asked, "What would you have been if your grandmother and grandfather had been donkeys?" The Methodist youth looked at him and said, "I guess I would have been a Baptist."

There was a lady that lived in a community where there was only a Catholic Church. It was the only church there, and she went. She loved God and she knew Jesus. She attended regularly and there came the time in her life when she was to die. The priest came by to pay her a visit. She was on her deathbed. The priest said, "I am so glad you attended our church, I only wish you had become a Catholic and had joined the Church. I could have prayed for you and forgiven you of your sins, and you'd go to heaven." She looked at him and said, "You don't need to pray for me. My sins are forgiven, and I am going to heaven." The priest looked at her and said, "Lady, don't you know that Peter holds the keys?" She said, "You tell him to keep the keys, I've got the door." Jesus is the door! Not the priest, not the preacher, not the church.

I don't tell that story to put a Catholic down. I love the Catholics, but I want you to know something: the only way the Catholics are going to get to heaven is through Jesus, the door. They are not going through the priest, Peter, or anyone else. I know a lot of Catholics and Baptists that have never met Jesus. Just because you have been christened or are a member of a church doesn't make you "saved."

How many of you have met this Jesus who changes lives completely? Jesus says, "Beware of false prophets, which come to you in sheep's clothing, but inwardly they are ravening wolves" (Matt. 7:15). Do you know that Satan will almost always disguise his prophets in sheep's clothing? They will be so slick and so smooth, subtle and smart. You'll say, "Boy, I like that." They will twist the truth. It only has to be twisted a little bit, then it becomes a lie. You can preach one truth as though it were the whole truth, and it becomes a lie.

One example of taking a truth and preaching it as the whole truth and making it a lie is this. Have you ever heard that God is love? Is God love? Is that a truth? Is that the whole truth? God is wrath, but you don't hear that. God gets angry. He says, "My wrath is revealed from heaven" (Rom. 1:18), and I don't want to go into the details, but I want you to hear this. God says, "When you know Me and don't glorify me as God, I am going to give you up." That is the judgment of God, a God of wrath. So we preach that God is love. God is the great love. That is all you hear. That is what the Mafia says, and every criminal says. God is also just and holy. You must be careful. There will always be prophets in sheep's clothing that will twist the truth. Paul called it perversion of the gospel. He called it double-doctrines and seducing spirits. We have them today. He said if anyone comes preaching to you any other gospel other than the gospel that I preach, let him be accursed.

There are those today who make light of the blood of Jesus Christ which was shed for your sins. They call that a bloody ole' religion. You are blood bought, friend. Every American is blood bought. Your liberty was blood bought. Every time the flag unfurls, at an athletic contest, every red stripe should remind you of blood that was spilled on the battlefield to buy your liberty. Someone died for you, and I guarantee you that the sons and daughters that died on battlefields fighting for your liberty were not fighting for the liberty of a bunch of people who parade all over America against our government and some in the name of homosexuality. They didn't die for that kind of liberty. God help them, and God forgive them. We are not to make light of any biblical doctrine. The Bible is the Word of God! There are those today who cast doubt on the Word of God. God in heaven inspired this Word. Don't let anyone cast doubt on the Word of the eternal God. There are wolves in sheep's clothing. You are going to know them by the fruit of their life.

I want you to hear what Jesus says to those who listen. "Not everyone who says to me, Lord, Lord, shall enter into the kingdom of heaven; but he that doeth the will of my Father which is in heaven. Many will say to me in that day," referring to the last day of judgment, "Lord, Lord, have we not prophesied in your name? and in your name have cast out devils? and in your name done many wonderful works? Then will I profess unto them, I never knew you: depart from me, you that work iniquity" (Matt. 7:21-22). Does Jesus know you?

Some say they know him. That is not the question. Does he know you? Read the last three verses in the second chapter of John, and you will find these words: "Many of them believed when they saw the miracles which he did" (v. 23). They believed when they saw the miracles. You are not to worship miracles. You are to worship the miracle worker, the Master! "You call me Master and Lord: for so I am"

(John 13:13). He said, "No man, having put his hand to the plough, and looking back, is fit for the kingdom of God" (Luke 9:62). He is the King of kings. He is the Lord of lords. They believed when they saw the miracles that he did, but John 2:24 says, "Jesus did not commit himself unto them, because he knew all men."

He knows your heart. He knows my heart. We all like spectacular things. We are living in a miracle age. I guarantee you a man can come to any city on the east coast and announce that he is going to have a healing campaign, and he will pack that building to the rafters. You can go in that same town and announce that you are going to have a meeting to preach the blood of Jesus and the cause of Christ, and you will have an empty building. Brother, we love the flesh. When we hurt physically, that is what we think about. We don't seem to understand that Jesus Christ left heaven and came to earth to redeem men's souls. The Bible says that Jesus came "to seek and to save that which was lost (Luke 19:10). Why don't we get caught up in what he is caught up in? We are still "bread and fish" worshipers, that's why. We are miracle worshipers. I believe in a miracle-working God. Mayo Clinic sent my mother home to die. Mayo Clinic said, "Ninety percent of your bone is infested with cancer. You cannot live, lady. All that we can do to help is to give you pain medicine." I want you to know that the great eternal God healed my mother of bone cancer, and my mother is seventy-five years old. She is a beautiful, lovely lady. God healed her.

After we left a crusade in North Carolina, I received a fantastic call from a man who told us how God gave him the faith to believe! He had a little girl who the doctors said was going to die. She couldn't hold her head up. Couldn't turn over. She was dying. They told him that there was extensive brain damage, no hope for her. He shared with his interim pastor what was taking place. The pastor said, "Get about four of the men you love and believe in and who love the Lord. Let's just pray for her." They met and prayed and asked God to heal her. Miraculously, God literally healed that little girl. She is a healthy, beautiful little girl. The doctors still do not understand it.

I believe in a God that heals people. Before I preached to 18,000 people at the Southern Baptist Pastors Conference, a pastor's wife gave her testimony. She was the only blind girl to ever go through Tennessee Temple Schools in Chattanooga. Shortly after she left the school, she and her husband were praying by the bed, and God miraculously gave her sight. She can see! The incredible thing is that the doctors examined her eyes and said, "You cannot see, your eyes are blind." She sees with blind eyes!

I believe in a God that heals people. Don't make light of that, my friend. Listen, there is something wrong with people who are so caught up in the miracle that they totally miss the Master. We have people running everywhere today looking for another miracle. They say, "Lord, look at all these works we have done." But he said, "I never knew you." Does he know you?

In Texas we have a lot of things we like to talk about. Someone said if you knock all the air out of a Texan, all you have left is a pair of boots and a hat. We Texans are real happy about some things we have in Texas, and one of the things we are happy about is the Dallas Cowboys. We like the Cowboys! We don't like them because Tom Landry is a Christian. We like them because they play football well. When driving around Dallas you see many bumper stickers on cars: Cowboys, Superbowl Champions, No. 1. You can ask people of Dallas, "Are you a Cowboy?" "Man, I'm a Cowboy, yes sir, I'm a Cowboy." You can ask them, "Do you ever go to the game?" "No, I listen to them over the radio or watch on television." They are not a Cowboy. They are Cowboy fans. Some take it dead serious. They get their popcorn and peanuts and cokes; their beer and pretzels, and they sit down in front of their television. They are not Cowboys, they are fans! Fans grab their kids; they grab their binoculars; they drag their kids to the arena with their $10 tickets; and they get fired-up! We do it right in Dallas. When you see the Cowboy game, you see these sweet, little things come out in their boots; and bless God, that is about all they have on. Here they come in their Cowboy boots, strutting out on the field, "We're Cowboys!" They are not Cowboys. They are Cowboy Cheerleaders, cheering on the Cowboys. I don't have any trouble telling the difference. They are not Cowboys.

Now, if you pay close attention, you will see one of these dudes come out on the field. He will have on a grey helmet, a star on it, big shoulders, streamlined from the waist down, and that dude will get down across the line and say, "G-r-r-r-r-r-r." When that ball goes "hut," they come unglued. He's a Cowboy. He is in the game. I want you to know that in Christianity today, we have more fans than you can count. They sit in front of the television, they have bumper stickers, and they have lapel pins on their shirts. Fans, that's all they are! Jesus does not know them.

I remember well when Arkansas was on its way to the finals in NCAA basketball. They had a black man that played for them who loved Jesus. *Sports Illustrated* wrote about him and how much he loved God. Melvin Delph! He loved God! I watched them annihilate Texas Christian University. I am not an Arkansas fan, I am a Texas fan. I watched them, and they were fine. After that game was over, those Arkansas fans piled down on the court. Many began to grab at those athletes, those stars. You could watch people grabbing at them, reaching out at them. I watched Melvin that night as he left the arena. Melvin pushed his way through the crowd. They were hollering and grabbing at him. He didn't look at them. One of my friends' son went to school with Melvin and played football at Arkansas. He loves God, and he and Melvin were buddies. He was in Ft. Worth to watch Melvin play that night, and they had not seen each other in awhile. Melvin was going toward the exit when all of a sudden, David came up from the right and reached out to Melvin. I saw Melvin turn, he looked, stopped, and pushed his way through the crowd to David. They embraced each other for a moment. "How are you doin', Man?" Everybody knew Melvin, but Melvin didn't know everybody. He knew David and he stopped.

One day a lady pushed through a crowd and touched Jesus. He turned and looked into the crowd and said, "Which one of you touched me?" "We all are, Lord," came the reply. "No, only one did. Where are you?" The lady fell down trembling and said, "Lord, I touched you." He knew her. It doesn't matter if you know him tonight. Does he know you? That is all that matters. Is he a person? Is he real to you? "Not everyone that says Lord, Lord, shall enter into the kingdom of heaven; but he that doeth the will of my Father which is in heaven" (Matt. 7:21-22). "Oh, but Lord," you say. "Not everyone that says, Lord will enter the kingdom of heaven." Does he know you?

I knew all about him. I knew enough that I joined the church, but I didn't know him. One night I had to come to myself and say that I didn't know him. I will never forget the night, 115 or 116 degrees in Pine Bluff, Arkansas, out under a tin shed in a rodeo arena. An outstanding group called the New Hope Singers sang for us that night. A young man was the assistant song leader and also the pianist. I gave the invitation and that young man got up from the piano and came and gave his life to Jesus. He said, "I knew what I was, and God knew what I was. I was a phony." That boy came to Jesus that night, and he is our pianist. Jesus can do it.

Back in March, on the Monday night after Easter, over 5,000 people were in Owensboro, Kentucky. Reba Ware was playing the piano so beautifully, as she always did. She had been working for me for years. She heard me preach many sermons. My staff and I had already met privately that night before the service and prayed for her by name. Something was wrong. We didn't understand it, but something was not right. God was moving so mightily in our team, but she couldn't get on track. She wasn't bad; something just wasn't there. The Spirit of God was moving and she couldn't seem to get on the wavelength. Everything was distant to her. We prayed for her. That night during the invitation, I was so disturbed for some reason, I didn't even want her to play the piano. She was the only one playing. Not even the choir was singing. People were getting saved. I just turned and looked at Reba and said, "Stop playing." She stopped, but didn't realize that I meant for her to stop playing the piano. She said that it was like the voice of Almighty God saying, "Stop playing, quit pretending." Right there on that piano bench, Reba Ware was saved. Our crusade pianist was saved. What a beautiful talent God has given her.

That night, going home to Ft. Worth, we were so happy! I gave her a verse of Scripture, and said, "Read this, Reba." She started reading, and tears fell from her cheeks and spattered on the Bible. She said, "I have read that a hundred times, but it never said anything to me before. It does now." "Not everyone that says unto me, Lord, Lord, shall enter into the kingdom of heaven" (Matt. 7:21). Many of us will say that we have played many, beautiful concerts in his name. We sang many solos and choir numbers, many specials. "Lord, we did many wonderful things," but he will say to you, "I never knew you." I can be honest with you here and now. I know that he knows me! I know him. I'm positive. I am so sure that I'm willing to walk out of here and die tonight, and never wonder one moment where I am going. There is no need for *you* to wonder because I know exactly where I'm going. I know whom I have believed. I know who I believe, and he knows me. Satan gives us so many substitutes, it is scary. Does he know you? Do you know him?

3
What in the World?

Jack Stanton

O Lord our Lord, how excellent is thy name in all the earth! who hast set thy glory above the heavens. Out of the mouth of babes and sucklings hast thou ordained strength because of thine enemies, that thou mightest still the enemy and the avenger. When I consider thy heavens, the work of thy fingers, the moon and the stars, which thou hast ordained; What is man, that thou art mindful of him? and the son of man, that thou visitest him? PSALM 8:1-4

One of life's great questions is the question of self-identity. Many are asking, Who am I? Where did I come from? Is this all there is to life? Is there life after death? Where do I go from here?

A famous actor was asked where he was going. His reply was, "How can I know where I am going? I don't even know who I am."

What in the World Are You?

Some will tell you that you are nothing. That you are a piece of protoplasmic scum floating on the cosmic surface. That you are an accident of nature coming from nowhere and going nowhere. This is about as intelligent as saying that a watch, keeping perfect time, came into existence when its numerous parts came out of nowhere and accidently formed into the intricate and logical sequence which makes up its delicate mechanism.

Others would have you believe that you are a bundle of integrated and interrelated chemicals, and that your life is

32

largely determined by chemical reactions. The human body is composed of many chemicals. The average person has enough phosphorus to make eight thousand matches which can be used for many useful purposes. This same amount of phosphorus can kill five thousand people, so you have within you the potential for good or evil. You have in your body enough carbon to make nine thousand three hundred sixty lead pencils; enough lime to mark off a baseball diamond; enough fat to make a fifteen-pound candle; enough iron to make a ten-penny nail; twenty spoonfuls of salt; sixty lumps of sugar and thirty-five hundred cubic feet of gas. You may be more heavily endowed in some of these areas than the average. Chemical reaction cannot produce love, forgiveness, freedom, or new life. There is much more to you than your chemical makeup.

Still others will tell you that you are the product of your environment; that you are boxed in by where you are and there is no escape. Some go so far as to say we are what we eat. I hope not! In a lifetime the average person will devour five calves, twelve sheep, ten pigs, eight thousand pounds of beef, seven thousand pounds of fish, thirty thousand eggs, six thousand loaves of bread and nine thousand pounds of potatoes. What kind of monstrosity would develop if we became what we eat?

Have you ever felt as if you were a bundle of nerves? You may have a right to feel this way. There are seventy-two feet of nerves in one square inch of skin. You have around nine million nerves in your body.

But you are more than any one of these or the sum total of all of these.

What does God's Word say about you? The Bible declares that God created man in his image. "So God created man in his own image, in the image of God created he him; male and female created he them" (Gen. 1:27).

You are a created being made in the image of God. You have been given will, intellect, and emotion that you might have fellowship with the Father.

But something happened. Man became disobedient and lost this fellowship with the Father. Living in disobedience, man began to experience loneliness, fear, and guilt. "And the Lord God called unto Adam, and said unto him, Where art thou? And he said, I heard thy voice in the garden, and I was afraid, because I was naked; and I hid myself" (Gen. 3:9-10).

Romans 5:12 declares, "Wherefore, as by one man sin entered into the world, and death by sin; and so death passed upon all men, for that all have sinned." Our condemnation comes not because of Adam's sin but because of our own sin. Romans 6:23 gives us the solemn warning that "the wages (the payment, the natural outworking) of sin is death."

Man, created by God, disobeyed God and stands under judgment for his sin. The good news for this bad situation is that God still loves us and has made it possible for us to have forgiveness of our sins and new life through Jesus Christ. "For God so loved the world, that he gave his only begotten Son, that whosoever believeth in him should not perish, but have everlasting life" (John 3:16). You are the object of God's love. No doubt you have many in your family and friends who love you, but no one cares as much for you as Jesus.

This leads to the second question.

Where in the World Are You?

I do not mean where are you geographically, but where are you in terms of history and meaning. What's happening in our world? What is it doing to you? Where do you fit in?

David Lloyd George is quoted as having said, "There are

times when the world travels at such a giddy speed that it covers the tracks of centuries in a year." You live in such a time. Our world has been described as morally rotten, socially diseased, politically corrupt, and spiritually anemic. Dr. Charles Howard describes the world as a woman heavy with child and asks will there be an abortion, a still birth, or a healthy child? He goes on to say that the world faces a revival, the return of our Lord, or ruin.

Ours is a day of great scientific advancement. We have walked on the moon, probed the great expanse of the universe, transplanted hearts in dying men, and have reached out toward physical life through DNA.

While we have made tremendous strides in the physical realm, we have stumbled in the spiritual. Many among us have lost their way, and the population explosion only compounds their confusion. We live in the midst of plenty, yet millions are starving. We live in an affluent society, but multitudes are in desperate need. We have an ever-increasing number of specialists to help us deal with our tensions, yet more and more people break under the strain of modern living.

We live in a secular world which tries to rule God out of the universe and thinks only of the here and now. An actress being interviewed on television stated that at the close of the program she and a man who was not her husband were going to Mexico and live it up. Aghast at her crude and suggestive statements, the interviewer reminded her of her husband and asked what such a trip would do to her marriage and her career. She replied, "I'm thinking only of the now." What a selfish, childish attitude! Is it still true that "God is not mocked: for whatsoever a man soweth, that shall he also reap"? (Gal. 6:7).

We live in an immoral world which flaunts its new morality which, in many cases, is the old immorality under a new name. Drunkenness, drug addiction, and divorce are three evils that continue to work great havoc in our midst. We live in a rebellious world which strikes out against all authority and tries to make gods out of men.

We live in an evil world where satanic forces are coming out more openly. A young girl told a pastor she wanted to have a child, kill it, boil it in water, and use the water in a communion service to the devil. Many persons feel that the increase of mutilated animals found in numerous places across our nation is evidence of increased devil worship. How evil can we get before God comes in judgment?

Where do you fit in? What crowd do you run with?

Unable to cope with life, some cop out through suicide or suicidal equivalents such as drugs, liquor, and illicit sex. These never satisfy but demand more and more excessive use to provide the previous stimulation.

Those hooked on drugs blow their minds and ruin their health. Many get to the place where they are so freaked out they are unable to speak coherently, too stoned to walk or even stay awake. Many who have found freedom from drug addiction and new life in Jesus Christ still are handicapped by frail health and mental limitations imposed on them by their previous continued use of drugs.

Liquor creates illusions causing a person to feel high. The string of broken lives, broken homes, bankrupt businesses, and fatal accidents that follows the use of liquor gives vivid evidence of its destructive force.

Illicit sex creates all kinds of problems. Billy Graham tells of a girl who claimed to be an atheist but when she returned to her apartment after a sex orgy would pace the floor saying, "I feel so dirty. I wish someone would say you are forgiven." A person who says before marriage, "prove your love for me by having sex with me" is not thinking in terms of love but of self-satisfying demands. Premarital sex is no proof of love but often creates a sense of guilt and shame, a doubt about the mate, and haunting memories. A survey revealed that college campus psychiatric problems are four times as high among girls who engage in premarital sex as among those who do not. God's Word is plain enough. "Flee fornication. Every sin that a man doeth is without the body; but he that committeth fornication sinneth against his own body. What? know ye not that your body is the temple of the Holy Ghost which is in you, which ye have of God, and ye are not your own? For ye are bought with a price: therefore glorify God in your body, and in your spirit, which are God's" (1 Cor. 6:18-20).

Drugs, liquor, and sex are all God given and useful in their rightful place. Sin is the misuse of God's benefits.

Some mob out. That is, they follow the crowd and use as the reason for their actions "everybody's doing it." God wants thinkers who will lead the crowd, not follow it. You are a unique person with God-given abilities. No other person can help the world in exactly the same way you can help it. Let God bless your life and use it to bless others.

Some flop out. That is, they give up. Life seems too much for them. They just quit. They learn to exist but they never really live. Ethel Waters was right when she said, "God don't sponsor no flops." God wants your life to be full and meaningful and he will give you the enabling power to experience that kind of life.

Why in the World Are You Here?

Or, what on earth are you doing for heaven's sake? God's gift to you is life; what you do with it is your gift to God.

> Brothers, I call upon you, by the mercies of God, to present your bodies to Him, a living, consecrated sacrifice, well-pleasing to God—for that is the only kind of worship which is truly spiritual. And do not shape your lives to meet the fleeting fashions of this

world; but be transformed from it, by the renewal of your mind, until the very essence of your being is altered, so that, in your own life, you may prove that the will of God is good and well-pleasing and perfect (Rom. 12:1-2).[1]

God asks you to present your body, all of you, all of your everyday activities as an act of worship. This, he declares, is the worship which is truly spiritual.

You must not let the fleeting fashions of this world mold your behavior. You are not to be conformed to the principles of this world which are centered on self, nor the practices of this world which say do the other fellow before he does you, nor the pleasures of this world which are sensual and degrading. You are to be in the world but not of it. You must be separated or distinct from the world but not isolated from the people nor insulated from their needs. You must be transofrmed from the world "by the renewal of your mind until the very essence of your being is altered."

"Let this mind be in you, which was also in Christ Jesus" (Phil. 2:5).

> Wherefore, my beloved, as ye have always obeyed, not as in my presence only, but now much more in my absence, work out your own salvation with fear and trembling. For it is God which worketh in you both to will and to do his good pleasure. Do all things without murmurings and disputings: That ye may be blameless and harmless, the sons of God, without rebuke, in the midst of a crooked and perverse nation, among whom ye shine as lights in the world; Holding forth the word of life (Phil. 2:12-16).

God has a purpose for your life. He loves you and wants the best for you. As you walk in obedience to his will you will find his purpose for your life. Let Jesus live out his life through you and you will find yourself busy in the world meeting the needs of others and finding the answers for the needs in your own life.

How in the World Can You Live the Victorious Life?

Jesus said, "I am come that they might have life, and that they might have it more abundantly" (John 10:10). That is, your life might be full and meaningful. How can a person live a happy, meaningful life in a crazy world like this?

To experience the victorious life you need pardon from your sin. This pardon provides forgiveness and freedom and is available only through Jesus Christ. "Who his own self bare our sins in his own body on the tree, that we being dead to sins, should live unto righteousness" (1 Pet. 2:24).

God commands, "Let the wicked forsake his way, and the unrighteous man his thoughts: and let him return unto the Lord, and he will have mercy upon him; and to our God, for he will abundantly pardon" (Isa. 55:7).

The Bible declares, "And this is the record, that God hath given to us eternal life, and this life is in his Son. He that hath the Son hath life; and he that hath not the Son of God hath not life" (1 John 5:11-12). Christ in you is the key to victorious living.

You also need peace, not the transitory peace the world offers but the inner peace that Jesus alone provides. Jesus said, "Peace I leave with you, my peace I give unto you: not as the world giveth, give I unto you. Let not your heart be troubled, neither let it be afraid" (John 14:27). And again he said, "These things have I spoken unto you, that in me ye might have peace. In the world ye shall have tribulation: but be of good cheer: I have overcome the world" (John 16:33). Even in a mixed-up world there can be peace of mind and serenity of spirit, for "the peace of God, which passeth all understanding, shall keep your hearts and minds through Christ Jesus" (Phil. 4:7).

Purpose is a vital ingredient of the victorious life. Direction and guidance are needed in the journey of life. The psalmist reminds us that, "The steps of a good man are ordered by the Lord: and he delighteth in his way" (Ps. 37:23). While the writer of Proverbs tells us, "In all thy ways acknowledge him, and he shall direct thy paths" (Prov. 3:6). God is a loving Father who will help you in all of life's important decisions.

Even if your sins were forgiven and you possessed an inner peace and you had established the right purposes, you would still need power to face the crazy conflicts of the world. This, too, is available in Jesus Christ. Jesus promised, "I will not leave you comfortless [an orphan]: I will come to you" (John 14:18). Paul reminds us that "God has not given us the spirit of fear; but of power, and of love, and of a sound mind" (2 Tim. 1:7). Power is available through the Holy Spirit, and the Christian is instructed to be "filled with [or controlled by] the Spirit" (Eph. 5:18). Jesus said, "Ye shall receive power, after that the Holy Ghost is come upon you" (Acts 1:8). The promise is "Ye are of God, little children, and have overcome them: because greater is he that is in you, than he that is in the world" (1 John 4:4).

Life can be full and meaningful through Jesus Christ. "He came unto his own, and his own received him not. But as many as received him, to them gave he power to become the sons of God, even to them that believe on his name" (John 1:11,12). Three words stand out in this text. They are believe, receive, and become.

Will you believe him? Believe that he is the Son of God who died for your sins and rose from the dead to put you right with God. Will you receive him? Ask him to forgive your sin and come into your life and control it. As you do, you will find that Jesus has given you the power (right, authority, ability) to become a child of his.

As one who has received Christ and has found that he will do all he promised and much more, I urge you to bow your head in prayer and turn your life over to Jesus Christ that he might be your Lord and Savior and make your life full and meaningful and eternal. May God bless you as you do it now.

---

[1]From William Barclay, *The Daily Study Bible*, "The Letter to the Romans" (Philadelphia: Westminster Press, 1957), p. 167.

4

How to Profit from Problems Through Promises

Mike Gilchrist

For unto us was the gospel preached, as well as unto them: but the word preached did not profit them, not being mixed with faith in them that heard it.   HEBREWS 4:2

But my God shall supply all your need according to his riches in glory by Christ Jesus.   PHILIPPIANS 4:19

Most of us shrink from the very thought of coming into need. Yet need is the door through which we walk toward discovery of God's vast supply. Every need should excite us. The very need signals that God's supply is at hand. He will certainly not permit us to experience any need for which he does not have a more than adequate supply. How do I know? Philippians 4:19 says, "But my God shall supply all your need according to his riches in glory by Christ Jesus." "All your need" is covered by the promise of God's "supply" from the abundant resources of his "riches in glory."

Thus, needs excite the maturing Christian who knows something of the faithfulness of God. These needs indicate a new discovery about to be made. What a contrast in attitude this will make to that of the immature. Instead of discouragement, there is delight. Not that we are oblivious to momentary human need but are more impressed by awareness of God's promised provision.

Hebrews 4:2 gives us the formula: "For unto us was the gospel preached, as well as unto them: but the word preached did not profit them, not being mixed with faith in them that heard it." It is even better understood when coupled with Philippians 4:19. Promises come alive and profit us only when there seems to be a problem, a need. Food never interests me unless I am hungry. Supply meets need. Where there is no sense of need, there is no search for supply. Likewise, promises cover problems. Where there is no consciousness of a problem, there is no quest for a promise. So problems are to send us shopping for promises in order to profit.

Now let us go to the Word of God to zero in on illustrative situations where this formula is spelled out in life experiences. Consider the case of the nobleman of Capernaum in John 4:46-53.

The problem is obvious. The boy "was at the point of death" (v. 47). To say the least, this is the type problem that gets a father's full attention. Nothing else seems to matter in a moment like this. The next business venture is unattractive. Social involvements are insignificant. The problem is preeminent. Undoubtedly he had exhausted all human resources. The finest medical minds and facilities available to the nobleman were employed only to fail. The boy was still dying. Then came good news. Jesus had performed a miracle at a wedding feast in Cana. "If he could change water into wine, he could heal my son," decided the nobleman. Quickly the father gathered his servants and began his journey to Cana. This was a "shopping" trip based on two convictions and a hope. First, the father was convinced that Jesus could heal his son, due to his past performance of the Cana miracle. Second, he had a great desire for Jesus to perform the miracle of healing his son. However, just because he believed he could and wanted him to, he had no assurance that Jesus would. Thus the journey was for a promise, a commitment from Jesus.

How many times have you and I known that the Lord could and desperately wanted him to but did not know he would, because we had not heard from heaven. We know nothing until we hear from heaven. We need a word from the Lord. That word from the Lord comes from the Word of the Lord, not from dreams or visions. So we begin a shopping excursion into the Word for a word which the Lord will make our own personal promise: his promise, for our problem, revealed to us by his Spirit.

When the nobleman reached Jesus in Cana, his first words were, "Sir, come down ere my child die" (v. 49). Then he awaited the reply. What would be the Word from the Lord? What would he hear from heaven? Then came the most beautiful words ever put together for his ears. "Go thy way; thy son liveth" (v. 50). This was the promise for his problem. The shopping expedition was a success! But wait! Now comes the crises! Hebrews 4:2 says, "The word preached them did not profit them, not being mixed with faith." The promise must be mixed with the problem by the cement of faith in order to profit. He knew Jesus could heal the boy. He wanted him to. Would he now believe the words the Lord had spoken to him? The evidence of his believing Jesus would be whether or not he acted accordingly. James says show me your faith by your works. This would be the cement for mixing the problem and promise for profit.

Perhaps some of us would have said, "So easy? So simple? I cannot believe it." We would have held onto Jesus, while the servants went back home to check the boy's condition. Not so with this father. Verse 50 tells us, "And the man believed the word that Jesus had spoken unto him, and he went his way." He believed and acted accordingly.

That completed the faith package. He had mixed the problem and the promise.

What about the profit? As he returned to Capernaum and approached his home, his servants came running to meet him saying, "Thy son liveth" (v. 51). There was the profit! "Then inquired he of them the hour when he began to amend. And they said unto him, "Yesterday at the seventh hour the fever left him" (v. 52). These words indicate an even greater and more far-reaching profit. A discovery had been made through this life situation. A spiritual formula had been realized for future situations. A faith relationship had been established between the nobleman and Jesus. Who can doubt the benefit of this problem? No problem, no promise, no profit. No need, no supply, no discovery of God's vast resources. Now it begins to make sense that need is to be the door of discovery.

Another illustrative life situation showing need to be the door of discovery is found in 2 Chronicles: 20. Word came to King Jehoshaphat of Judah that the enemy was approaching in awesome numbers. Humanly speaking, there was no way of taking on such odds. His first response was the normal human emotion of fear, "And Jehoshaphat feared . . ." (v. 3). This emotional response triggered the spiritual formula that followed, as always is the case with a mature believer. Jehoshaphat instantly related the situation to God. He "set himself to seek the Lord, and proclaimed a fast throughout all Judah. And Judah gathered themselves together, to ask help of the Lord" (vv. 3-4). Why? The king and his people knew the Lord could save them. They certainly wanted the Lord to save them. However, they knew that was not enough. They could not sit passively on those two facts and hope for the best. They needed a specific promise for their problem; a word from heaven, a contract from the other world. The quest for a commitment began.

"O our God, wilt thou not judge them? for we have no might against this great company that cometh against us; neither know we what to do: but our eyes are upon thee" (v. 12). They waited for a word. It came.

"Thus saith the Lord unto you, Be not afraid nor dismayed by reason of this great multitude; for the battle is not yours, but God's. To-morrow go ye down against them . . . . Ye shall not need to fight in this battle: set yourselves, stand ye still, and see the salvation of the Lord with you, . . . fear not, nor be dismayed; to-morrow go out against them: for the Lord will be with you" (vv. 15-17). There it was; the promise for their problem. But wait! Would they mix the promise with the problem by faith for profit? That they did.

"And Jehoshaphat bowed his head . . . all Judah . . . fell before the Lord, worshipping . . . to praise the Lord God of Israel with a loud voice on high" (vv. 18-19). They believed God in their spirits. But there is a further step. Would they act out in their volition what they believed in their spirit? Would they show their faith by their works? Did they believe God sufficiently to act accordingly? God required this by saying, "To-morrow go ye down against them." This was the acid test of faith. No shallow believism would suffice here. The defeat of the enemy by the living God would have to be a settled fact, as though already accomplished, for them to march into the faces of this multitude pouring down upon them.

The answer? "He appointed singers unto the Lord . . . . They went out before the army, and to say, Praise the Lord; for his mercy endureth for ever. And when they began to sing and to praise, the Lord set ambushments against the children of Ammon, Moab, and mount Seir, which were come against Judah; and they were smitten" (vv. 21-22).

Jehoshaphat and the people were so confident in the faithfulness of the Lord to keep his promise that the king sent the choir marching ahead of the army in the praise of faith to sing of God's faithfulness. As the walls of Jericho fell, when the children shouted their praise of faith, so this pagan army fell as the Lord cast upon them a spirit of confusion causing them to destroy one another. When the battle is the Lord's, an army is not necessary—only a song! When the promise was mixed with the problem by faith, there was great profit!

Now let us face a different fact. Searching for a word from God does not always produce the specific promise we desire. When it does not, however, God always has something better. Paul made that discovery according to 2 Corinthians 12:7-10.

Paul had a problem, "a thorn in the flesh" (v. 7). He asked the Lord for a promise, "I besought the Lord thrice, that it might depart from me" (v. 8). The promise he received was not the one he requested. The word from heaven was better. It came in a twofold promise:

1. "My grace is sufficient for thee" (v. 9). God promised Paul that the thorn would be a heavenly pipeline through which God's grace would flow into his life in greater measure than he ever dreamed.

2. "My strength is made perfect in weakness" (v. 9). God promised Paul heavenly power in exchange for human weakness.

The great apostle made his choice. He sided with God. He chose God's grace and heaven's power over the removal of the thorn. He cemented the promise to the problem by faith when he said, "Most gladly therefore will I rather glory in my infirmities, that the power of Christ may rest upon me .... for when I am weak, then am I strong" (vv. 9-10). Is there any doubt that he (and we through him) profited greatly?

Perhaps you are now saying, "How do I know when I get

a word from God?" God will see to it that you know. You will also know that you know. This is the work of the Holy Spirit in you. No man can do this work for him. It is his ministry within your human spirit.

Perhaps you are also asking, "How do I exercise faith in the promise for the problem?" The answer is simple. The same way you did for salvation. You had a problem. You were a sinner separated from God and lost, "For all have sinned, and come short of the glory of God" (Rom. 3:23), and "Whosoever shall call upon the name of the Lord shall be saved" (10:13). You reached out in faith to Jesus joining the promise to your problem and counted so what the Word of God declared to be so. You confessed it to be. "With the mouth confession is made unto salvation" (10:10). Acting upon and confessing the promise sealed it to the problem for great profit, salvation!

This basic principle which God teaches us in the hour of our spiritual birth is the fundamental upon which he intends for us to operate all the days of our lives. "As ye have therefore received Christ Jesus the Lord, so walk ye in him" (Col. 2:6).

5

The Doctrine of Adoption

Sam T. Cathey

*Now I say, That the heir, as long as he is a child, differeth
nothing from a servant, though he be lord of all; But is under
tutors and governors until the time appointed of the father.
Even so we, when we were children, were in bondage under
the elements of the world: But when the fulness of the time
was come, God sent forth his Son, made of a woman, made
under the law, To redeem them that were under the law,
that we might receive the adoption of sons. And because ye
are sons, God hath sent forth the Spirit of his Son into your
hearts, crying, Abba, Father. Wherefore thou art no more a
servant, but a son; and if a son, then an heir of God through
Christ.* GALATIANS 4:1-7

*For ye have not received the spirit of bondage again to fear;
but ye have received the Spirit of adoption, whereby we cry,
Abba, Father.* ROMANS 8:15

I had just closed a revival meeting and had come home to
reacquaint myself with my wife and children and to rest.
That particular Monday my pastor's little daughter was in a
hospital for delicate surgery, and he was with her the entire
day. In the afternoon a lady called me and said, "Brother
Sam, our pastor is at the hospital, and a lady called me from
a trailer park saying that a man there is in need of a
preacher. I thought of you and wondered if you would go." I
drove to that trailer park, inquired where the man was,
found my way to the rear of the park and knocked on the
trailer door. A man came to the door with a wanton, empty
look on his face. The minute I looked into his eyes, he cap-
tured my attention and love.

He said, "Come in. Are you the preacher?" As we sat down, he twisted his hands and said, "Now, Preacher, I've been drinking. I won't lie to you. I've been drinking, and I'm an alcoholic. But, Preacher, I'm not drunk, and I want you to know that. I know what I'm doing. I'm at myself. I've been drinking but I'm not drunk. Do you believe me?"

"Yes, sir, I do," I said.

He said, "I've come to the end of the row. I can go no further. I have to have help, and I know that God is the only one who can help me. Preacher, will you tell me about God?"

Oh, would I tell him! Did I tell him! I told him everything I knew to tell him and did it with joy. You see, when you begin talking about the Lord, you relive the blessedness of Christ in your own heart and the thrill of knowing him as your own wonderful Savior. I told him about my Lord. I tried the best I knew to tell him that when one believes in Christ Jesus, Jesus gives the sweet liberty and the freedom from whatever it is that has one in bondage. He then believed with all his heart and said, "I want this. Would he have me?"

"Would he have you? He stands ready and anxious to come into your heart and life, if you will only believe him. If, like a child, you'll believe it, not only will he save you, Roy, but he'll deliver you from the power of the shackles of alcoholism."

He literally fell from that couch to his knees. Humbling himself, he bowed until his face and clenched hands were touching his knees. In that unimposing, unimpressive little trailer, he looked just like a clump of rags. That undeserving man got hold of God, and God got hold of him. He was wondrously saved that afternoon!

After we had talked for a few minutes, Roy said, "Preacher, before you go, I want to do something. I want you to stay while I do it."

Roy walked into the kitchen of that trailer and opened the refrigerator. It was full of beer! He reached in, got a sixpack, tore the box away, opened that beer and poured it down the drain. Again and again, he would reach in and get another sixpack. One by one, he opened the cans and poured them down the drain. It was the first time in all my "put-togethers" that I rejoiced in seeing somebody "pop-a-top." The fact is, I wanted to get in on it, too. As he was poppin' the tops and pourin' it down the drain, I would reach in and get another sixpack and hand it to him. There was joy that day as he emptied over two cases of beer!

Roy stood back and thought for a moment. He reached into the cabinet above the sink, brought down a bottle of whiskey, snapped it open and poured all of it down the drain. Next, from behind the refrigerator, he got another bottle of whiskey and opened it and poured it down the drain. Again, he thought a moment, and said, "The old woman doesn't know about this one," and reached up under the table and jerked. Tape gave loose and a bottle appeared. This, too, he opened and poured out.

He said to himself, "Is that all? No!" He went back to the bedroom and found a partially filled bottle and poured it down the drain. Then, he went into the living room, reached up and under the couch, pulled out a wad of cotton stuffing, and got another bottle. Grinning at me, he said, "She didn't know about this one, either." He poured it down the drain.

This is what I really want to tell you! I went outside and was ready to leave. Roy was leaning up against the door of the trailer. He looked at me, and with a deep soberness, said, "Preacher, am I really God's son?" Nonchalantly, I said, "Why, of course you are." He said, "You mean really?" I replied, "Well, of course you are God's son." "Preacher, you mean I'm really God's son?"

Then, all of a sudden, it hit me. It came overwhelmingly fresh to my own soul—"God's son!"

I was made to realize what had really transpired there in that little insignificant, unimposing trailer. A man fell to his knees and told God about his sin and his degenerate state. God, in his infinite love and by a strange, mystical power, birthed that man into the family of God. Literally, not figuratively, not theoretically, literally, that man was born into the family of God.

The Bible plainly says in Galatians 4 that when a person believes, he is liberated from the power of sin and literally comes to be a son of God. This gives him the privilege of saying, "Abba, Father."

The exact meaning of "Abba" is not known. All that is known is it is a term of respect; it is a term of love. It is never used unless there is a deep love and respect for the one to whom it is expressed. It is always used of a man in an eternal relationship with his God. God tells us that through Jesus Christ we are adopted into the family of God. Through Christ we receive the spirit of adoption that enables us to say with love, devotion and tenderness, "Abba, Father."

I said, "Yes, Roy, you are a child of God." I stepped back into the trailer and read Galatians 4:1-7.

Then I read Romans 8:15.

"And now, Roy, when I leave and you close that door, turn around in this room, lift your face to God, and with humility say, 'Abba, Father.' He will understand and know that this is the most honorable and most blessed expression of your heart. He will know it comes from the tender affection you have for what he has done for you."

Later he told me he did this.

The most blessed experience any man has ever undergone is that wonderful moment, that tremendous experience, when he is born into the family of God. By the sovereign grace of God, and not by the works of man, we are made to become the sons of God.

Roy came that night and presented himself as a candidate for baptism into the fellowship of our church.

One evening I went to a lovely home in Plymouth, Michigan, and greeted an impressive, good-looking young man. He had educated himself and worked hard. He had come up in the ranks of an insurance company and was now twenty-seven years old. All around him were the obvious evidences that he had been a studious and diligent individual.

As I sat talking with him, I noticed that he kept looking around the corner into the next room where I heard noises. I knew there was a little child back there. "Sir," I asked, "are you babysitting for Mama?"

"Yes I am," he said, and indicated apprehension for the child.

I told him I would like to see his child. That was all he was waiting for. Off he went and brought back the baby. I wish you could have seen the glow on the man's face. I wish you could have seen the fatherly love and happiness and thrill etched on his face as he sat there and bounced that little boy on his knee.

"My wife and I couldn't have any children. We wanted one badly so we adopted this little boy," he said.

Here was my opportunity to talk to this man about Christ. "Sir, do you know you cannot disinherit this child?" He looked at me quizzically and I continued. "That's right. You cannot legally disinherit an adopted child. That child is your child now and forever. When God wanted to explain to you and me what it means to be the son of God, he used the imagery of adoption. In order to become a Christian, you must be adopted into the family of God in the same way this boy was adopted into your family."

The young father asked, "Do you mean that?"

At this point I read to him the Scripture where the apostle Paul said, "We are adopted into the family of God."

Let me explain the imagery that the Word of God wants us to see. There was a legal transaction at the time of Christ called the *patria potestas.* Our word *father* is derived from the Latin word *patria,* and "testament or statement" is derived from *testas.*

In the time of Christ there were not many orphans, for there was a clannishness among the people. It had to be an extreme, abstract case for there to be an orphan. But when an orphan was found, the unusual, legal transaction of adoption transpired.

The historical significance of adoption, in the time of Christ, is exemplified when a man found an orphan and inquired of the orphan if he would like to become his child. If the answer was yes, a courier announced to the city that there would be an adoption. The prospective father would then take the child into the court square. He would put one hand on the head of the child, lift the other hand to the sky, and announce three times, *patria potestas!*

The first time he said *patria potestas,* he was saying to the witnesses, "From this moment on, this child's past is wiped out." The second time he was saying, "From this moment on, this child's identity is changed and he assumes mine." The third time he was saying, "This child's future is guaranteed, and my belongings become his inheritance." The moment that transaction closed, it was over and finalized. All three of those monuments of that experience came into living, vital reality, never to be altered and never to be changed.

God wants us to understand clearly what it means to be his child. Therefore, our Bible takes the picture—the imagery—of the *patria potestas* and records it as the same thing that happens when you are born into the family of God.

You literally, not figuratively, not theoretically, not with any form, not even the suggestion of supposition, but literally, become the son of God for time and for eternity. When you confess your sin, when you repent of that sin, and when you receive Jesus Christ by faith into your heart, the Holy Spirit of God, by the mystical, magical power of the grace of God, converts you into the family of God. You receive, literally and definitely, the spirit of adoption. This is unalterable. This is the gift and this is the grace of a great and glorious God toward us who are so undeserving.

Who of us does not need our past obliterated? How many of us have said, "I'd like to be a Christian, but, Preacher, you don't know what kind of person I've been"?

A prostitute may say, with tears running down her face, "I want to be a Christian, but God can't forgive the horridness of my sin."

The man waiting on death row might say, "I want to be a Christian, but can God forgive a man who has murdered?"

A potential murderer might ask, "Can God forgive a man who has murder in his heart?"

A little child might tenderly inquire, "In my heart I am such a sinner. Pastor, can God save a boy like me?"

A faithful, dedicated, loyal mother may say, "I've tried to be an honorable mother, but I have failed by not being a Christian. Can God forgive that kind of sin?"

What is there about you that separates you from God?

When God adopts you into his family, the Bible says he gathers up all the sin of your past and casts it behind his back to remember no more. Society may not forget, but God will. He will wipe out your past and everything that bothers you. He will wipe out every burden of your heart and every anxiety and perplexity of your mind. Our blessed, wonderful Lord will eradicate and erase, instantly, the moment you give the entry: "Yes, I want to be the child of God." By the adoption of the Spirit of God, your past will be wiped out.

How many are those who have said, "I want it. You Christians seem to be so happy. I want to get in on it, but I am afraid I can't hold out."

"I'm afraid I can't live up to it."

"I know me; I know my desire for alcohol."

"There is still evil desire im my heart."

The Bible says when you are adopted into the family of God, God changes you. You become a new creation in Jesus Christ. You are going to think differently and desire differently. There will be a complete change in your life that will reestablish motivation and will recreate a sense of value. There will be within you the desire for godliness in the same way that there is within you, now, the desire for worldliness. God will do that for you.

One time a man said to me, "Do you Baptists really believe that once you are saved you are always saved?" I said, "Yes, we believe it because the Bible teaches it." He asked, "Now, do you mean to tell me you believe a man can be saved and go out and do anything he wants to and then die and still go to heaven?" I replied, "I sure do. I believe a person can really get saved—really get saved! Any man can really be born into the family of God, really become the son of God. I believe he can do that and go out and do anything he wants to and go to heaven." The man said, "I wish I could believe that!"

"Sir, we Baptists understand and believe the Bible teaches that when a man really becomes the son of God and is really born into the family of God, God changes his 'want to.' "

When a person is born into the family of God, there will be a change in him. He will not want the things of this world.

The Bible says if the love of the world is in a man, then the love of God is not. There are a lot of church members today who are going to die and go to hell because they only joined the church but have never been adopted into the family of God. They have never released their lives to God. When a person becomes a child of God, God changes that person. His identity is changed. Literally, Jesus Christ comes into his life and makes him a new person. He is changed for the express purpose of glorifying and honoring God in his life.

Don't reject Christ because you are afraid you can't live right, or because you are afraid you can't live godly, or because you are afraid you will be a hypocrite. If you will allow God to adopt you into his family, God promises, on the authority of his Word, you will have a new identity.

Finally, the Bible teaches us, in the imagery of adoption, that all of the inheritance of our Father becomes ours. Christians are joint heirs of Jesus Christ in all the eternal glories of heaven. All the things our minds can't imagine are ours because of the gift of God.

If you would trust Christ, he will guarantee your future of a home in heaven. He will give you the seal and sign of his promise that you will never again be lost. You will never be deserted by God. Jesus is now preparing a mansion for you so that where he is, there you may be also.

As Christians, Jesus is our brother, because we are the children of God. All the inheritances of heaven are ours. Everything that has come into existence, by the hand of God, is waiting to be inspected and enjoyed by us. We are the recipients of the grace of God because we have deliberately and volitionally let Jesus Christ come into our hearts and lives.

To have this future, all we have to do is trust Christ. We must give our hearts and lives to Jesus Christ and let the blessed power of God adopt us into his family. By the infinite love of Christ, we may have our pasts obliterated, our identities changed, our futures guaranteed, and the inheritances of God. This promise of God is wrapped in his love.

We know only human love. If you let God have your life, you would know infinite, eternal, divine love.

Recall, now, the imagery of adoption. Only one thing could stop the transaction. Caesar could not stop it. Litigation could not stop it. There was no statute that could stop it. Josephus, the first-century historian, said the only way to prohibit adoption was if the child said, "No! I do not wish to be your child!" The only thing that stops you from becoming a Christian is to openly say to God, "No! I do not want to be your child!"

There are many reasons and excuses for not becoming a Christian. Basically and essentially one is saying, however, "I don't want to be your child." A person might say, "Not now. Maybe later." In the mind of God, this person will have said no.

Is what you think important? or God, and how you have treated him? He wants you to be saved today. He loves you! He loves you in spite of your past, in spite of your identity, and in spite of your bankruptcy. He wants to wipe out your past, change identity, and give you the wealth of eternity.

In Texas there is a home for children called "Buckner's Orphanage." The founder is affectionately referred to as "Daddy Buckner." One day he went into the little girls' compound and some forty children rushed to him. He took time to love and kiss each of them. He looked across the grounds and there, up against a bush with her face turned away, was a little girl who had not come to him. He asked the lady in charge why she had not come. The lady answered, "Dr. Buckner, she has a terribly scarred face from a burn. She thinks she is ugly and is ashamed. She thinks you wouldn't love her."

The story is that Daddy Buckner walked over to that child and got down on his knees. She turned her face from him, but he looked at her and said, "Honey, why didn't you come to love Daddy Buckner?"

"You don't love me. I am ugly," was her reply.

"Sweetheart, what makes you think you are ugly?"

"You haven't seen my face. It is ugly!"

Daddy Buckner reached out, picked her up, and tenderly turned that little face all the way around until he could see it. He planted at least a hundred kisses on that scarred face.

Oh, what love is that! Oh, what tenderness is that!

But it cannot compare with a God who can look down upon the ugly and scarred ruin of our soul. He saw our soul, tainted by sin, and yet loved us so much that he said, "I want you to be mine! I want you to be mine! I want you to be my child. If you will let me, I will adopt you. You will be mine forever!"

You must decide.

6

The Logic of the Gospel

Angel Martinez

For by grace are ye saved through faith; and that not of yourselves; it is the gift of God: Not of works, lest any man should boast. EPHESIANS 2:8-9

[1]Next to man's love for sin, the crowning transgression of this apathetic age is man's stunning ignorance of spiritual things. Even people who have repeatedly heard the gospel are in the dark concerning the things "that accompany salvation." The gospel is simple; it has depth, but it also has breadth. It is within the reach of every human being who desires to be saved. Paul told the men on Mars' Hill that they should "seek the Lord, if haply they might feel after him, and find him, though he be not far from every one of us" (Acts 17:27). Paul said, "You can feel after him." In other words, something that you can feel after is not far from you. The apostle said, "God is not even that far; you can feel after him." You cannot stretch your hand in any direction without invading God's territory. One of the most condemning features of the judgment is going to be the fact that the gospel was so simple that "the wayfaring men, though fools, shall not err therein" (Isa. 35:8), and yet men stumble around it into hell.

Jesus had this same problem to contend with in his day. You recall when he was conversing with Nicodemus, that brilliant Jewish lawyer, how it amazed him that this Pharisee did not understand the rudiments of grace. Jesus knew what was in man, but in this conversation with Nicodemus, one finds the Lord a bit surprised and somewhat chagrined because of this man's inability to comprehend simple spiritual truth. We find this evident in the question in John 3:10: "Jesus answered and said unto him, Art thou a master of Israel, and knowest now these things?" You see, Nicodemus had his M.I. (Master of Israel), but he did not have his B.A. (Born Again). Here was this man, with more degrees than a thermometer, and yet he was oblivious to the "wind that bloweth where it listeth" (3:8).

In John 4, we find the same lament on the part of Christ concerning the woman at the well. When the Lord spoke to her about the water of life and its subsequent effect upon her person, she dove into a theological discussion concerning the traditions of the mountain on which men ought to worship. She was lost in the suburbs of truth; Jesus got her back to the essentials when he remarked, "If thou knewest the gift of God, and who it is that saith to thee, Give me to drink; thou wouldest have asked of him, and he would have given thee living water" (v. 10). But she did not know.

The apostle Paul had a similar experience with his people. Hear him cry, "Brethren, my heart's desire and prayer to God for Israel is, that they might be saved. For I bear them record that they have a zeal of God, but not according to knowledge. For they being ignorant of God's righteousness, and going about to establish their own righteousness, have not submitted themselves unto the righteousness of God" (Rom. 10:1-3). They were ignorant in the day of Paul, and human nature does not change. People in this day know so little about God's way of redemption. You can engage any person in conversation concerning the matter of salvation, the open Bible, and the active church and it will amaze you how illiterate people are about the way to God. Most people think that God is keeping score on every person, and every time one does something good, the Lord puts it down on the right-hand side of the ledger, and every time the person does something wrong, he puts it down on the left-hand side, and then, when the individual dies, God draws a line underneath and adds them up, and if the good deeds exceed the bad ones, he goes to heaven, and if the bad deeds exceed the good ones, he goes to hell. Nothing is further from the truth than that, and yet the majority of people will try to make the wheel of salvation revolve around the hub of human merit.

In our text, we have the word *works* mentioned twice. In verse 8 works are condemned, and in verse 10 works are commended. Why the change? Let us not overlook the importance of order in God's way of dealing with the human race. In fact, almost all of the errors that arise in the realm of spiritual thinking are due to a reversal of God's order. For example, in Matthew 6:33 Jesus said, "Seek ye first the kingdom of God, and his righteousness; and all these things shall be added unto you." But man comes along and reverses that and seeks things first, and places God in second position, where God will not function, and then wonders why his whole life is disordered.

Take another example, the Roman Catholic plan of salvation. Mark 16:16 states, "He that believeth and is baptized shall be saved; but he that believeth not shall be damned." The order is faith and then baptism. The Roman Church reverses this statement and baptizes the infant without any faith and infers that the baby has been washed from original sin. The Bible states that only a believer can be baptized; the baby has no capacity for faith, hence the infant is no fit subject for baptism. This matter of changing God's order has been clearly manifested in many of my revivals. Jesus said in Matthew 18:3, "Verily I say unto you, Except ye be converted, and become as little children, ye shall not enter into the kingdom of heaven." A little child comes down the aisle to be saved; after the service, the parents rush to the front and begin to quiz the child in adult fashion and expect the child to give adult answers, and if he does not, they claim that he does not know what he is doing. They try to make the child into an adult, when Jesus said the opposite. He said that the adult should become as the little child.

In my study of the Bible and the plan of salvation, I have uncovered to my own satisfaction, three statements that summarize the structure of the way of redemption. The gospel is the most logical thing in the world. That is why Isaiah could say, "Come now, and let us reason together" (Isa. 1:18). That is why Paul could reason with Felix and Drusilla on "righteousness, temperance, and judgment to come" (Acts 24:25). If you can grasp these next three statements, I believe you will have the logic of the gospel in a nutshell. First, we are not condemned by works; second, we are not saved by works; third, we are not kept by works. As I have mentioned, works are condemned in verse 8, while they are commended in verse 10. In verse 8 they are condemned because there is an attempt to make them the root of salvation. Works are not the root of salvation; they are the fruit; they are not the requirements of salvation, but rather the results. In verse 10 we find them in place, hence we are created unto good works. I want to dwell in my outline on the three words, "Not of works."

I. We Are Not Condemned by Works

Many people believe in salvation by grace, but condemnation by works. It is important that we remember that we are not condemned by works. Men don't go to hell for being bad, nor do they go to heaven for being good. Christ is salvation and condemnation. Men go to hell because they reject Christ, and they go to heaven because they accept him. In John 3:18 we find these significant words, "He that believeth not is condemned already, because [note that] he hath not believed in the name of the only begotten Son of God." The Bible does not say that he was condemned because he got drunk, or because he committed adultery, or because he gambled or even murdered; he was condemned because he did not believe in Christ. Now, mind you, these things mentioned are bad, but they are not sufficient to damn the soul. These things may keep a man from coming to Christ, but not coming to Christ is what keeps life from the soul.

If God sends men to hell primarily for their moral sins, then God is unjust. If God sends men to hell for getting drunk, God is unjust. If God puts men in hell for committing adultery, then God is unjust; if God hurls men to hell for gambling, then God is unjust. It would be as unjust to send men to hell for any of these things mentioned as it would be to put a man in the penitentiary for life because he stole a loaf of bread or ran a traffic light. I say that in either case the penalty would be out of proportion to the crime. And it is this that unsaved people do not understand. Hence, they entertain the idea that if they stay away from the grosser sins, they will be saved. If you were to pick up your morning paper and read in the headlines that a certain man was sentenced to the electric chair, you would immediately surmise, without reading the details, that whatever the person was guilty of must have been horrible because, as we have said, men are not sent to the electric chair or the gas chamber because of a misdemeanor.

When I read in my Bible that men are going to hell, I conclude that whatever they have done must be awful to merit such punishment, terrible and eternal. I discover in my Bible that men do not go to hell for moral sins because Jesus atoned for those on the cross. Then I discover that they go because of their unbelief and their refusal of the saving grace of Christ. Beloved, it must be an awful sin to reject Christ. It must be worse than murder, Christ can forgive that; it must be worse than gambling, it must be worse than adultery. Rejecting Christ is the worst sin that men commit. Think of it; the worst sin that a man commits is not in the gambling casino; it is not committed in the night club; it is not committed in the house of ill fame. Believe me, it is committed in church when pastors give invitations and sensible men will spit in the face of God and aim their gun of unbelief and fire at the person of Christ on the cross. If I could impress you with the awfulness of this sin, you would not sit unmoved; you would tremble like a leaf in a storm; you would bite your lips until the blood ran; you would clench your fists until the bones cracked.

That's why men go to hell; and they should go, if the depravity of the heart is so entrenched that human beings can refuse the marvelous mercy of the seeking Savior. Often people ask me if I believe in the depravity of man. And I answer that I certainly do. Why do you believe in man's depravity, they ask, because he gets drunk and comes home and beats up his wife and children? No, as bad as that is, that is not the proof. Because man fights and kills his fellowman? Again the answer is no. Because man drops atomic bombs on innocent women and children? Again, I answer no. Those things are bad and horrible, but the real proof to me that man is utterly ruined and depraved is the fact that you have to beg him to be saved. Have you ever heard such a contradiction? If a man was famished for water out in the scorching desert and I was to come with a pitcher of cool sparkling ice water, do you think that I would have to beg that man to drink? He would knock me down in the attempt to get the water. If a man was starving, and was I to bring him to a table laden with the best food that money can buy, do you think that I would have to say, "Please, my friend, you are starving, eat a few bites, they will help you?"

You smile, but that is the plight that we face in dealing with the human soul.

In my travels up and down the country, I have found many young people disturbed about hell. They wonder how there can be such a place. They often bring their interrogations to me and ask, "Did you ever have any trouble with the doctrine of hell?" I have been to college and seminary; I have read books of every type, and have been exposed to infidel literature and books on philosophy, but I can honestly say that I have never doubted hell. Why should I doubt that men go there who reject Jesus? I have never had any trouble with hell; we all deserve to go, we have sinned against God, we have trampled underfoot the blood of the covenant wherewith he was sanctified, we have done this despite the spirit of grace; we deserve to go. But I will tell you what has given me trouble. Heaven has given me trouble; that is the greatest mystery to me. How can God take a vile, corrupt, unworthy sinner and in one instant put a new man within the suit without unbuttoning the coat? How can God take the scum of the earth and transmute it into a gem for heaven. That's the thing that puzzles me. But it is true, praise God. He can save to the uttermost, or as John McNeil, the great Scotch preacher, used to say, "He can save to the guttermost."

We are all condemned by the fact that we have refused the Lord of mercy. Often I hear people say that man is made in the image of God. That is not so. Man is not made in the image of God; he is made in the image of Adam. Adam was made in the image of God, but Adam defaced the image and he bequeathed to the human race the tragic results of that fall. Only after we become Christians will we have that image restored. That is why it is so essential that we accept Christ; that is why he left the halls of glory for the nails of Golgotha. There is no other way to be saved; Christ is the remedy.

II. We Are Not Saved by Works—Not of Works

If it is true that we are not condemned by works, it is also true that we are not saved by works. If men could be saved by their own efforts, then Jesus would never have had to die. Paul said, "I do not frustrate the grace of God: for if righteousness come by the law, then Christ is dead in vain" (Gal. 2:21). This is a very important truth; it is at this juncture that denominations divide. There are many who are trying to mix in human effort, but in so doing, they rob themselves of the help of Christ. You cannot afford to put a plus sign by the blood of Christ. The only way a man could be saved without becoming a Christian would be for that person to live a perfect life from the time that he is born until the time that he dies. He would have to be perfect. Don't you see, that is why it is impossible for a man to be saved on the strength of his character and goodness. The only way it could be done would be for that person to be perfect, and there is no such achievement in the realm of human effort. Christ was perfect, therefore he needed no savior and could become a savior. The blasphemous doctrine of the Roman Catholic Church that Mary was born perfect, called the Immaculate Conception, is not supported by the Word of God. In Luke 1:46-47 we have these words from Mary's lips: "And Mary said, My soul doth magnify the Lord, And my spirit hath rejoiced in God my Savior." Mary said that she needed a savior; only sinners need saviors, therefore Mary was a sinner.

God is a perfect God. No one would question that. The only way that God can receive us, is for us to become perfect. You heard me right, friend of mine; the only way that we can ever be saved is for us to become perfect. But, you

say, that leaves all of us out of the picture because we are all
sinners, and none of us is perfect or can become perfect.
You are right; but there are two ways to acquire perfection;
we can earn it or it can be given to us. Now we are all aware
of the fact that we cannot earn it, for we have all sinned. The
only other way we can acquire perfection is for it to be given
to us. This is where Christ steps in. Jesus came to earth and
lived a perfect life and died on the cross to redeem us from
our iniquities. Now he comes to every sinner and wants to
give his perfection in exchange for our sins. That's right,
becoming a Christian simply means that we trade our sins
for the righteousness of Jesus. We take his heaven and give
him our hell. He goes to a cross because of our sins, we go
to heaven because of his perfection. That's the logic of the
gospel; it is the most reasonable fact on the face of the earth.
How men can reject it is beyond the comprehension of this
preacher.

A sinner is a person who has sinned at least one time.
"For whosoever shall keep the whole law, and yet offend in
one point, he is guilty of all" (Jas. 2:10). A sinner is anyone
who is less perfect than God. According to the Bible, we
have all sinned. Often, when I go visiting, I find men confused as to their true condition. We will go into a person's
home and hear him say, "Why, preacher, I am as good as
those folks at the church where you are preaching; if they
make it, I will." For all these years that I have been preaching, I have been looking for one honest man to say, "I am as
bad as those folks in that church, and I need to do something about it." Instead, they will dilate on the good things
that they have done, and like the Pharisee who went to the
Temple and bragged on himself before God, they remain in
the same condemnation. We need the spirit of the publican
who said, "God, be merciful to me a sinner" (Luke 18:13).

Here is a startling truth; the unsaved man can do nothing

to please God. In Proverbs 21:4 we have these words, "The plowing of the wicked, is sin." Think of it; the Bible says that when an unsaved man plows, that is a sin. Well, what's wrong with plowing? Isn't it supposed to be good? When the unsaved man does it, that is a sin. The unsaved can do nothing good before God. Every time that the unsaved man gives to charity, in the sight of God, that is a sin. When the unsaved man takes part in civic progress, that is a sin; when the unsaved man is good to his neighbor, that is a sin; when the unsaved man lives a good, moral life, that is a sin. Oh, you say, that's putting it mighty strong. That's what the Bible says. I know that this is a hard blow to the goodness of man, but if the good man could only realize how bad his goodness is when he refuses to be saved, I do not believe that he would persist in this hellish course. The Word of God also puts it this way, "But we are all as an unclean thing, and all our righteousnesses are as filthy rags; and we all do fade as a leaf (Isa. 64:6).

Let me illustrate this truth just mentioned. Suppose that you are invited to eat at a person's house, and this individual has a contagious disease. Let us imagine that she makes a fruit salad. She may use the best recipe and the best ingredients that money can buy. What is wrong? When she puts her hands in the mixture, she ruins the whole thing. But, you say, this is a good fruit salad; it contains the best ingredients. It is ruined, however, and it is not fit to eat simply because the person mixing the salad has a foul disease. And so with the sinner. He is contaminated by the virus of sin, and everything that he touches, he contaminates; when he plows, he contaminates the plowing; when he lives right, he contaminates good morals. The natural man cannot please God.

So we have all sinned, and the only way that we can be saved is to accept the perfection of the Savior. The good,

moral man can never make it because he is not perfect, that
is why the Lord Jesus is indispensable to the plan of salvation. God's admission price is perfection and every one of
us falls short. Some of us may come closer to it than others,
but the standard is inflexible; thus, we are all doomed. As we
stand there reflecting upon the inadequacy of human merit,
the Lord Jesus Christ comes and says, "What's the matter?"
We reply, "We would love to be saved, but we don't measure up because we are not perfect." Then Jesus offers his
perfection and if we accept it, we enter into the kingdom on
the merits of another.

How wonderful is our Lord Jesus Christ. How criminal
for men to refuse such a simple and reasonable provision.
Man will have a difficult time facing this rejection at the
judgment. When Christ died on the cross, he prayed,
"Father, forgive them; for they know not what they do"
(Luke 23:34). Friend, he cannot pray that prayer for you,
because you know what you are doing. You are insulting
the Lord of glory; you are hardening your heart against the
Holy Spirit, and you are doing it in this day when the Bible
is open and churches invite you to learn of Christ. On such
sinfulness, the verdict of the judge will be final. There will be
no appeal to a higher court. You shall stand condemned by
your own choice. Then flee to Christ. There is no salvation
within the confines of your own character. Don't substitute
your goodness for the perfection that God requires. The
worst kind of badness that a man can be guilty of is goodness without Christ. When you substitute your goodness for
the salvation of the Lord Jesus, you sin in the worst fashion
that is humanly possible.

God wants you to trust the Lord Jesus. Nothing that you
do will please him until you accept him as your Savior. The
other day a young lady said to me, "Tell me what Baptists
believe; I have been to the Catholic priest and to other

denominational leaders; I need a religion, and I am looking for one that suits me." I said, "Young lady, let me stop you right here and say this, don't you look for a religion that pleases you, you look for one that pleases God." It is amazing how people think that they are the center of this business of salvation. Our part is pleasing God and doing what he commands. We are the rebels; we must be willing to capitulate on God's terms. The only way we can please God is to accept his "only begotten Son."

Suppose my little eight-year-old son is kidnapped. In frantic desperation, my wife and I would do all within our power to trace his whereabouts. While in the process of the search, the phone would ring, and at the other end, I would hear this voice saying, "Mr. Martinez, we are the kidnappers; we have your boy and he is safe, but we plan to keep him. To compensate for his loss, however, we are going to place a million dollars in the First National Bank in your name, and furthermore, we will give you a new Cadillac every year." Now, you parents, need I ask you what answer would be given? With breaking heart I would say, "Listen, keep your money and your gifts, bring my boy back. I would rather live in perpetual poverty the balance of my life than to be without him." That is the way God feels about his only begotten Son. Your good works and good deeds are an insult to God. He wants you to accept the Lord Jesus as your Savior. Oh, if I could make you see this, you would run in haste to be saved. You would not continue to break the heart of God; you would not harden your heart against the one who delights in your salvation and who at this moment postpones his second coming so that you may come into repentance.

III. We Are Not Kept by Works

Let me call your attention to the third proposition. We

have stated that we are not condemned by works, and we are not saved by works. Now we come to an equally important point; we are not kept by works. Now here we part company with the people who believe in the "gospel of struggle." Many of our fine friends believe in salvation by grace and preservation by works. Now don't misunderstand me, works have their place, but as we said in the introduction, they are the fruits of salvation, not the roots. A child of God works for the Lord, not in order to be saved, but because he has been saved. He works for the Lord not in order to stay out of hell, but in order to take others to heaven. We are saved by grace, but we save others by works. I often hear folks say, "This world is a lifetime job preparing ourselves for heaven." That is wrong, I was as ready for heaven one minute after I was saved as I am right now, after preaching for twenty years. The duty of the Christian is to get others ready for heaven.

A Christian is saved by grace, and he is kept by grace, not by conduct. When God saves you, he forgives your sins from the cradle to the time that you accepted Christ. The Bible says, "The blood of Jesus Christ, his Son cleanseth us from all sin" (1 John 1:7). If he cleanses us from all sin and pays on the cross for all of our sins, how many sins are there left for us to pay? The answer is none. Believe me, Christ has forgiven the sins I will commit in the future just as he has forgiven the ones I committed in the past. I repeat, salvation is not contingent upon conduct. Oh, but you say, if I believed that way, I would get saved and then get out and live as I please. My friend, it doesn't work that way. When the Lord Jesus Christ, in his infinite grace and power, stoops to save, and the sinner comprehends the nature of his exodus, he becomes grateful and does his best to honor the Lord Jesus. I heard the story once of a preacher who walked up to a little black boy and said, "Do you mean to tell me that you believe in once saved, always saved?" The boy replied, "I sure do." "But son," continued the preacher, "what if you slip through his fingers?" "I cannot slip through," the chap replied, "I am one of the fingers."

I contend that in great matters of Christian doctrine, many people get lost in the suburbs of a truth, and they fight skirmishes on the periphery, so that they never discover the full implications that some positions finally lead to. For example, we are told in the Word of God that our names are written in the Lamb's book of life. If that be so, then every time we sin, those names have to come off. For example, let us say that John Jones of Memphis, Tennessee, puts his faith in Christ. All right, an angel in heaven puts his name down. The next time John Jones sins, that name has to come off. Then John Jones confesses and the angel puts it down again; then John Jones has a fuss with his wife, so the angel takes his name off, confesses again to God and his wife, and the angel has to put the name back on. That angel must have some arm; writing, recording, and erasing every time we confess and then sin again. For, you see, it only takes one sin for a man to be lost after he is saved, if it be true that he can be lost. How ridiculous! Brother, there are no erasures on the Lamb's book of life. God puts the name down and it stays there!

This is the most wonderful message that God ever gave to men. The devil has engineered a subtle strategy in getting men to hate and neglect this wonderful offer of full mercy. But, oh, what a price he paid to make it possible for us to have full salvation. "Forasmuch as ye know that ye were not redeemed with corruptible things, as silver and gold, from your vain conversation received by tradition from your fathers; But with the precious blood of Christ, as of a lamb without blemish and without spot" (1 Pet. 1:18-19). The cross reveals God at his best; it reveals man at his worst. The cross proves that God loves men; it also proves that men hate God.

[1]This sermon is from the book, *Revival at Midnight* by Angel Martinez. Copyright © 1956 by Zondervan Publishing House. Assigned to the author, 1974. Used by permission.

7

Resurrection . . .
Fact or Fiction?

Jim Wilson

And if Christ be not risen, then is our preaching vain, and your faith is also vain.   1 CORINTHIANS 15:14

Jesus Christ is risen from the dead! He is what? I said, Jesus Christ is risen from the dead! That statement was blasphemous to the Jews with all their religion. That statement was ridiculous to the Greeks with all their wisdom and understanding. That statement was subversive to the Romans with all their political power. Jesus Christ is risen from the dead.

I want to ask you, do you believe it? We all say we believe it. We celebrate Easter every year; however, I believe we live in a day when every individual who hears the claims of Christ is going to have to make a judgment of what is real and what is unreal, of what is true and what is untrue, of what is defeat and what is victory.

We talk a lot about victory. Bear Bryant, football coach of Alabama, has said, "Show me a good loser and I'll show you a loser." The basketball player speaks of an 88 to 87 score in an overtime game as the margin of victory. The football player says that 7 to 6 in a Super Bowl game is just enough to win. The politician speaks of 50.1 percent of the vote as enough for victory. We talk about victory and defeat in every realm of life, but for the Christian, victory is summarized in a single statement: He is risen from the dead! It is on this statement that all of Christianity really rests. That statement is the crowning point of our revelation. That statement ought to be examined by every man, woman, and child, regardless of his walk in life.

A theologian from Germany said that he believed in the meaning of the resurrection, but he did not believe in the fact of the resurrection. I don't believe that a man can really know my living Jesus and believe that! This man is a theologian, and he writes books about the Bible. He is held up in some circles as one of the greatest, but I don't believe any man who does not believe that Jesus arose from the grave can really be a follower of the living Lord!

Could our theology be based upon a myth? Could it? There are folks who say that it is. Could it be that all we believe about Jesus, the living Savior, and that all of this theology of the cross, his resurrection, and everything we hold dear, was given to us by some misguided fishermen who lived 2,000 years ago and none of it is really true? Could that be? It is time that the claims of the Christian faith be brought into court and put on trial for their validity.

"He is risen!" cries the Christian. Is it true or false? It is upon this claim that the whole of Christianity rests. What about it? Have the minds of men through the ages been polluted and undermined by the false claims of a misdirected church of 2,000 years ago? Or is the claim true?

Courtroom

The court is called to order. The defense attorney stands. "Your Honor, we will seek to show that the man, Jesus Christ, is the Son of God, that he came in the flesh 2,000 years ago, and that he broke into history as a man. But he was not just a man, he was God! He was not half God and half man, but he was fully God and fully man! Our finite minds cannot understand that concept, but we are going to seek to prove the fact that Jesus came as the God-man. We are also going to seek to establish the fact that he went to the grave, he rose from the dead, and he lives today; and that philosophically, historically, and experientially, people can know this living Jesus. Your Honor, I'm going to call some witnesses to come and give their testimonies.

First Witness

"We call a banker to take the stand. Sir, what do you have to say about this man Jesus whose followers said, 'He is risen'?"

The banker speaks, "Oh, yes, Jesus. I understand that claim. You see, my business is money. Like everyone of us here, I have debts, obligations, and responsibilities which I have not met, and penalties and fines which I cannot pay. In the time of tight money, I can realize what it would mean for someone to take a mortgage, pay it off in full, put it in a public place and write across it *Paid in Full* for the whole world to see. Your Honor, that's what he did for me. I'm not mortgaged at all. I owe no debt, except my life to Christ. He took all my debts, all my penalties, and all my fines; and he paid them in full! Your Honor, the Bible tells me that I, along with everyone else, was born in sin. All my life I had a tendency away from God and towards myself. I've never fought God or rebelled against him, but I've discovered that there are two ways to sin. One is by active rebellion, and the other is by passive indifference. I've just been indifferent to God so much of my life. I've gone my own way and done my own thing and left God out. Oh, I went to church on Sunday, and I'd pray every now and then, but I just didn't really live in God's power. Then Jesus lifted the burden and the sin and the guilt. He came into my life, and my life was changed! You see, your Honor, he took all this ugliness and all of this dirt inside me and just swept it away and made me clean. Even though I'm still a sinner, even though I still don't deserve God's grace, he's offered me a home in heaven, and I can live forever! Your honor, that's so exciting to me! Nineteen-hundred years ago, before I was even born, Jesus knew me.

> Jesus paid it all,
> All to him I owe;
> Sin had left a crimson stain,
> He wash'd it white as snow.
> ELVINA M. HALL

"That's the reason I'm a Christian. Jesus died for my sins. Yes, he died on the cross. His shed blood provided my salvation!"

This witness took his seat, and now the defense lawyer calls a prominent attorney to take the stand.

Second Witness

"What about it, Sir, how would you plead the case for this man, Jesus?"

The attorney speaks, "Well, obviously we all agree that historically a man by the name of Jesus lived. We would also agree that he died. His body was put in a grave somewhere, and we would agree that the body was missing. Now, the question before this courtroom, your Honor, is 'What happened to the missing body?'

"First, let's assume that the enemies of Jesus stole the body. Then, suddenly, the Christians, thinking that the body had legitimately risen from the dead, began to go up and down the streets and cry aloud, 'He is risen! He is alive! He is a living Savior.' They got such a magnanimous group of followers together that it became a threat to the Roman government. Your Honor, all those enemies needed to do, was to produce the body and to call a screeching halt to every person who followed this dead Messiah. They would have proved every Christian publicly and privately a fool.

And, as Christ's enemies, that is just what they wanted, but it never happened!

"The second alternative is that the followers of Jesus took the body. That's what the guards of the tomb were paid to say. The chief priests and elders feared that Jesus' followers would come and take the body to claim afterwards that he fulfilled his own prophecy. They went to Pilate and said: 'We want guards to watch the tomb. We are aware of his prophecy, that he will rise again the third day, and his followers may try to take his body.' The guards said, 'They came and stole him away.' Never mind the fact that his followers were so crushed by his death that they went back to their fishing boats with no thought of victory. Never mind how those few people could have rolled away a stone five feet in diameter. Never mind how they got past the trained soldiers of Rome. Never mind how on earth they pulled it off! His own followers took the body? Human nature being what it is; realizing that they had followed a fraud and having in their own possession a dead body, and then, because of their false claims, facing the possibility of having their skins removed while they were still alive, of being burned, and being fed to the lions, wouldn't they have produced the body and called a halt to their own fraud?

"Your Honor," says the attorney, "neither of these positions is tenable, and it leads me to the third alternative. It happened just as his followers claimed. Under his own power, the dead Jesus walked out of the grave, alive! That's what I think of Jesus! As a lawyer, I would have to say that logic leads to only one conclusion, he is risen!"

This witness takes his seat.

Third Witness

The defense attorney again steps forward: "Your Honor, you've heard these witnesses, but now I call a philosopher to take the witness stand."

"What, sir, do I, as a philosopher, have to say about the claims concerning Jesus?

The philosopher speaks, "Jesus, yes, I've studied him and his claims with great interest. I've determined that Jesus was either a man totally unique among all men, or he was a liar, and a cheat, and a con artist, and the biggest propagator of lies this world has ever known! Your Honor, he was not just a good man who was diluted because he made some very intelligent claims.

"I, as a philosopher, have imagined and envisioned the ultimate good, but I have never been able to live up to that standard. I've never been able to divorce myself from unrighteousness, from immorality, from basic selfishness and from a spirit of nonforgiveness. That is why Confucius, in an honest moment, said, 'The essence of what I have taught, I have not been able to perform.' Every philosopher points to an ultimate good, but never to himself. When Plato died, Plato was still searching. When Buddha died, Buddha said, 'I'm still seeking.' Your Honor, Buddha never claimed to be God. But he said, 'I'll show you an eight-fold path that will lead you to the state of nirvana.' However, he never told his followers that he was God. Muhammad never claimed to be God. He said, 'Allah is God, and Muhammad is only a prophet.' Your Honor, I look at Jesus in the middle of all this philosophical talk, and hear him say, 'I am the way, I am the truth, and I am the life. No man comes to the Father, but by me.' Your Honor, I examine the life of this Jesus and see one standing before a compulsive, opposing mob, challenging them to name one sin he has ever committed, one act of unrighteousness, one display of self-centeredness, and the mob is silent!

"I, as a philosopher, can't oppose a life that proclaims boldly and publicly, 'I do always (not sometimes, not nearly always, but always) the will of my Father!'

"No philosopher can miss the point that Pilate, the man who decreed Jesus' crucifixion, stood in front of the crowd with Jesus and said, 'I find no fault in this man.' Your Honor, I cannot oppose a life like that. That's the reason I'm a Christian!"

This witness takes his seat.

Fourth Witness

"Your Honor, this investigation would not be complete without calling on a historian to share with us his finding. As a scholar of history, what, sir, would you say of Jesus?"

"Your Honor, I recall all the fantastic personalities that have attracted and led men throughout the ages. Julius Caesar claimed to be God and made people bow down and worship him. The people bowed down and worshiped him, but they didn't really believe he was God. As a historian, I take note of the fact that no man alive today, including the Romans, worships Julius Caesar. Churchill, for all leadership, is today, unfollowed by any man. Abraham Lincoln, with his words of wisdom and truth and the admiration for him through the years, is today, only one to remember. He is not followed by men. He is dead. He is only a memory.

"For me, as a historian, your Honor, I must take note of the fact that of all dead leaders, only one is followed today in the conviction that he is alive! Only one is able to change lives. Your honor, Jesus has taken men who are weak, shiftless, and divided in their loyalty, and has made them strong, clean, and victorious. He's taken families who were divided: husbands who didn't love their wives, wives who couldn't tolerate their husbands, and children who would not obey their parents, and Jesus has come in and made that family a citadel of warmth, love, and fellowship. Your Honor, he's taken men who were slaves to drugs and has set them free from their slavery. He's come in and made them a new person. Your Honor, he's taken greedy, grasping, selfish men and made of them spiritual men. Your Honor, no mere mortal can change a man on the inside like that. It's only God's work! These people will tell you that Jesus is alive. He's a man who dates our history, before him and after him. He divides history! All you have to do is look at Jesus and see that there is no one like him before, and no one like him since. He's the God-man. That's the reason I'm a Christian."

The curtain closes on the courtroom setting and it brings us to the present.

Perhaps, you are thinking about these thoughts of victory, yet your life seems to be racked with defeat, uncertainty, boredom, and pressures from your job and circumstances. It seems that even as a nation, we are headed for moral and spiritual defeat. The world, I believe, is looking for a victory note that is struck with perfect tone.

When I think of victory, I so often think of Brian Sternberg. He was supposed to be the greatest pole vaulter ever, as he entered the Olympics of 1960. He was one of the ten best men in the world on the trampoline. Preparing for the Olympics, he was going through a simple routine on the trampoline, a double flip with a twist. As he came down, he landed on the edge of the trampoline. His neck broken and his spinal cord severed, he now lies in a hospital bed in Seattle, Washington. He has no hope of recovery or of moving a muscle. The doctors say he feels the terrible numbness, the excruciating numbness, as he watches his body wither away.

Despair? Defeat? No, you see Brian Sternberg, some months earlier, had been told about Jesus, the living Lord, who became his personal Savior. He smiles the smile of victory and says, "Life is not easy, but for me, life is Jesus Christ. Life and Christ are synonomous. They are the very same thing. That is the reason I can smile. The Christian life is not easy, but it's a life of joy."

How pitiful it is for any of us to see the victorious Jesus with the stone rolled away, and for us to insist on rolling the stone back for another year, as though he is dead, as though he is not risen, as though this Jesus is only a remembrance. While he was alive, before his physical death, he made the statement that was the crowning point of our faith. He said simply, "I am the resurrection!" And once he was dead, he proved it by rising. Now, I call on you to come and take the witness stand. What do you have to say about Jesus and for the claim of his followers?

After the second World War, the world was in rubble. All the leaders of the free world came together in a place called the Parliament Building in London, England. They began to discuss how they could reconstruct society. They offered all kinds of dreams and goals for the world. After three days, a young man of Oriental background came to the microphone, and his voice rang out like the voice of freedom. He said, "Gentlemen, may I have your attention?" Instantly, the entire Parliament Building got very quiet. This young man seemed to have an urgency in his voice. He said, "Gentlemen, I've been listening to your debates, your political legislation, your reformation programs. I want to ask you a question. As we've talked about peace for the world, have we forgotten the Prince of Peace, the Lord Jesus Christ?"

Somehow in the midst of our society, I believe that question has been lost.

The Scripture says: "Whatsoever is born of God overcometh the world: and this is the victory that overcometh the world, even our faith" (1 John 5:4). "And if Christ be not risen, then is our preaching vain, and your faith is also vain" (1 Cor. 15:14). "You are yet in your sins" is why we cry aloud for the world to hear: "He is risen!"

8

What Is a Christian?

Bill C. Penley

That if thou shalt confess with thy mouth the Lord Jesus, and shalt believe in thine heart that God hath raised him from the dead, thou shalt be saved. ROMANS 10:9

In 1929, the Rose Bowl game was being played between California and Georgia Tech. The game was as close as you'd want a game to go. It came down to the climactic moments. The score was 7 to 6. California was winning on their home soil. Georgia Tech had the ball, threatening to score, needing only a safety or a field goal to win the game. Every person in the stadium was alive. California fans were standing, screaming, "Hold that line! Hold that line!" Georgia Tech fans were chanting, "We need a touchdown! We need a touchdown!"

Suddenly, Georgia Tech fumbled. The captain of the California team, Roy Reigle, grabbed the fumble. Georgia Tech flew in on him, battered him and spun him around, but never did get him to the ground. He found a hole and raced through it as hard as he could go. There he was, out in the open, running with all his might for the goal posts. But there was a big problem: he was headed the wrong way! He had become disoriented, confused, and was running toward his own goal line. His teammates were yelling at him, "Stop, you're going the wrong direction! Turn around!" The roar of the crowd drowned out their warnings and on he went. His own teammates were after him, and one of the more agile

84

men caught him and dragged him down on his own one-yard line.

Well, they had the ball, maybe they could get a first down, a little bit of running room. In vain they tried three downs, and on the fourth down they had to kick. Georgia Tech broke through the line and blocked the punt, covered the ball in the end zone, got two points for a safety, and won the game. California lost the Rose Bowl game, 8 to 7, all because Roy Reigle had run the wrong direction.

But, friends, don't be too hard on Roy because he's not the only person who has made such an irretrievable mistake. There are millions of people in a game far more important than the Rose Bowl game, the game of life. They are running, running, racing toward the goal line of life; but all the time they are going in the wrong direction. At last, when the end of the game of life comes, and the final whistle blows, they realize that all the time they've been running the wrong direction.

My friends, to me this is the saddest thing I know. I believe this is the one thing that drives me on in evangelism, keeps me going. There are so many well-meaning people people who want to go to heaven, who are putting forth all their effort and energies trying to get to heaven, but all the time going in the wrong direction.

I would not venture to tell you how many times I've heard people say, "Well, Preacher, I think all of us are trying to get to heaven, but are just trying to get there on a different road." The Bible teaches there is only one way to heaven, and that's Jesus. He said, "I am the door: by me if any man enter in, he shall be saved" (John 10:9).

The purpose of this message is to answer the question, "What is a Christian?"

The word *Christian* has been misused, abused, and confused by many people who have had no right to try to define it. Most of us can't give a logical, clear definition of what a Christian is. I am not going to give you the definition according to Webster's Dictionary, for I have the real authority, and that's the Bible. Let's open God's Word and see what a Christian is.

I. A Christian Is One Who Has Made a Choice

The word *Christian* is only found three times in the Bible. The first place is in Acts 26:28. Paul stood before King Agrippa and preached right out of his heart telling him how to be saved. At the end of his message he gave the invitation: "King Agrippa, believest thou ... ?" (26:27). And Agrippa said, "Almost thou persuadest me to be a Christian" (v. 28).

Paul looked him straight in the eye and said, "I would to God, that not only thou, but also all that hear me this day, were both almost, and altogether such as I am, except these bonds" (v. 29). Paul told Agrippa that to be almost a Christian is to be altogether lost. He asked Agrippa to make a choice, to choose "whom you will serve."

You aren't a Christian because you were born into a Christian family. You aren't a Christian because your mother and father prayed for you. You aren't a Christian because you joined the church and were baptized. You aren't a Christian because you reformed your life. You aren't a Christian because you refrain from doing evil things. You are a Christian because you refrain from doing evil things. You are a Christian because, and only because, you have chosen Jesus Christ to come into your life, and by faith, you have invited him to come and live inside you.

He says, "Behold, I stand at the door, and knock: if any man hear my voice, and open the door, I will come in to him" (Rev. 3:20).

Have you had some specific, definite time in your life when you've invited Jesus Christ to come in and be your Savior? If you haven't, you aren't saved.

The question logically comes up, do I have to remember when I had that experience? I've heard the old mountaineer preacher say, "Bless God, if you can't remember the time and the place, you're just not saved!"

I don't agree with that at all. Maybe you can't pinpoint the exact time and place. Perhaps it was when you were only a small child, and as you got older you forgot that definite time and place. Or maybe you just don't remember things as well as you used to, for some reason or other. But there had to be a definite time, and I ask you, can you say right now, "I know I have asked Jesus to come into my heart. I believe right now that he lives in my heart and life?"

God has promised in his Word, "If thou shalt confess with thy mouth the Lord Jesus, and shalt believe in thine heart that God hath raised him from the dead, thou shalt be saved" (Rom. 10:9).

Have you believed in your heart, do you believe right now? Have you confessed Christ with your mouth? A Christian is one who has made a choice. You can't be neutral.

Nobody else can make the choice for you. Father and Mother can't make it for their children. Children can't make it for their parents. Your pastor can't make it for you. You have to make the choice.

In the tenth chapter of Mark's Gosepl we read about a rich young ruler who heard Jesus was coming to town. This young man came to Jesus as he walked along a road, and he fell down on his knees at the feet of Jesus and said, "Master, what must I do to be saved?"

The Bible records that Jesus looked at him and loved him. Jesus always loves sinners. Jesus told him what he had

to do to be saved. He reminded him of the Commandments. The rich young ruler said, "Master, all of these I have
kept from my youth."

I believe the young man was sincere, a good fellow.
Jesus, looking at him, loving him, answered, "You lack only
one thing." Here was a young man who had kept the law,
honored his father and mother, and all those things, but
Jesus said, "One thing thou lackest: ... come, take up the
cross, and follow me" (Mark 10:21). This young man got up,
turned his back on Jesus, and went away sorrowful.

Will you repeat this scene? Jesus, looking at you, loving
you, is stretching his arms out to you, inviting you to come
to him. The door is wide open. He says, "Him that cometh
to me I will in no wise cast out" (John 6:37).

Will you continue to reject the Savior? Make the choice! If
you haven't chosen Jesus, choose him right now.

II. A Christian Is One Who Has Been Changed

The word *Christian* in the Bible is in the book of Acts
11:26. It says: "The disciples were called Christians first at
Antioch."

Antioch was a wicked, pagan city. They didn't know
about God. An evangelist had gone there and told them of
the love of God in Christ, and a few of them had been
saved. These few formed a little church and were baptized.
They formed a fellowship together, and their neighbors and
friends began to notice their lives which had been so dras-
tically transformed. They said: "We will call them Christians." Because of Christ and because of their Christlikeness
they were called "Christians."

So you see that a Christian is not only one who has made
a choice, but one who has been changed! Now I am not
referring to a change that you make in your life. Not at all.
Sometimes when a person makes a profession of faith and

joins the church, he says, "Well, I have made a change." The Bible teaches us it is "not by works of righteousness which we have done" (Titus 3:5); "For by grace are ye saved through faith; and that not of yourselves: it is the gift of God: not of works" (Eph. 2:8-9). The change the Bible speaks of is not what you do. God makes the change for us, from the inside.

You may say, "I'm going to quit cursing, and quit drinking, and I'm going to start doing good. I'm going to start going to church, giving what I owe the Lord financially, and I'm going to start giving my life to God."

That's not the change the Bible is talking about. The change the Bible tells about is what happens when you realize with simple faith that you are a sinner and that Jesus died for every sin you've ever committed, that he went to the cross and suffered eternal judgment, damnation, the hell we deserved to suffer; and when we believe that Jesus, after he died for our sins, rose again, and is now seated at the right hand of the Father.

We open the door, as a choice, and then Jesus literally comes down on the inside of us in the person of the Holy Spirit. When God comes into these fleshly bodies of ours, he makes the change for us, from the inside.

Every one of you, if you're honest, will attest to the fact that you have things wrong in your life that you've tried time and time again to reform, and you can't. Right? And you'll never do it, because the flesh is depraved, at enmity against God, and the only way anything's going to be changed in your life is when you open it for God from the inside to do for you what you can't do for yourself.

You don't even help God, either. When you start helping, you hinder God.

Paul, in Colossians 1:27, said it is "Christ in you, the hope of glory." When you invite Jesus to come in, the first thing he does is save you and then he makes a new creature out of you.

Ezekiel 11:19 says God puts a new heart down inside you. Day by day God begins working on the inside of you, making of you the person he wants you to be, not the person you want to be, or your husband or your wife wants you to be, or your pastor wants you to be, but the person God wants you to be.

There are three categories of professing Christians. There is a group of people that I call "man-made Christians." You ask one of these people, "Are you a Christian?" He answers, "Oh, yes, my mother and father were Christians." Or you might get this answer: "Well, I'm a member of the Baptist church." Or "I'm a member of the Catholic Church." Sometimes, "Yes, I'm a Christian, I belong to the Masons."

All that person can tell you is what some organization or some person has done for him. Man-made Christianity will not take you to heaven.

Then there are "self-made Christians." You ask them, "Are you a Christian?" They may answer, "Oh, well, I try to keep the Ten Commandments." Or, "I try to obey the Golden Rule. I always try to do to others as I want them to do to me." "Yeah, I'm a Christian. I've quit this; I've begun doing that." You see, these people have a standard set up in their minds. They feel that if they can ever climb up and meet that mental standard they will be Christians. That won't take them to heaven.

The only way to heaven is "God-made Christianity," and that is when you, by faith, ask Christ to come in, and God, in the person of the Holy Spirit, comes down into the inside of you and makes out of you what he wants you to be.

My little girl, Tia, has a horse who walked between two small trees up in the mountains. His body went through, but his hip bones lodged, forbidding him from going completely through. He entangled his front feet in some wild grape vines. She didn't discover his plight for three full days. His body dehydrated, he had lost about 200 pounds, rubbed the hide off his flank, and was almost dead when she found him. Because I was away in a revival meeting, some of my mountain friends tried to doctor him with mountain remedies. They made a potion of sulphur and burnt motor oil and applied it. The next day the horse was no better. Then they fried some pork fat with a heavy mixture of salt and rubbed that on his wounds.

The following day I returned home, finding a horse more dead than alive. I called the veterinarian immediately. He came to my house, and in amazement looked at the horse, with drooping head and buckling legs. He simply stared at the poor animal and said to me, "Preacher, what on earth have you been doctoring that horse with?"

"Oh . . . ," I said, "We've put some sulphur and burnt motor oil on him; and some salted pork grease. We mountain men know how to doctor horses pretty well, but it seems we haven't helped him any!"

"You dumb preacher!" he exclaimed. "Don't you know you treat a horse like that from the inside?"

"No sir, I didn't know that."

"Well, now you do!"

He took a large needle, filled it with medicine, and injected it into the horse's neck vein. He charged me $35.00 and drove away. Next day I was amazed to look out to see the horse running around in the pasture, and drinking from the creek. He was well, cured!

I learned from that episode that there are diseases in a horse that all the doctoring you want to do from the outside won't heal. You've got to go to the inside.

God tells us in his Word that there's a disease in man in which all of our efforts to clean up on the outside are no good. That disease is sin. We can only be cured by an injection of the blood of Jesus Christ.

A Christian has been changed—changed by the blood of Jesus. Jeremiah says it this way: "Though thou wash thee with nitre, and take thee much soap, yet thine iniquity is marked before me, saith the Lord God" (Jer. 2:22). Only the blood of Jesus, my friend, can wash away your sins and change you.

III. A Christian Is One Who Has Accepted a Challenge

The third and last place the word *Christian* is found in the Bible is in 1 Peter 4:16. It says that a Christian is one who has accepted a challenge. He has made a choice, he has been changed, and has accepted a challenge: "If any man suffer as a Christian, let him not be ashamed."

A Christian is one who says, "I am willing to take Jesus Christ as my Savior. I am willing to wear his uniform. I am not ashamed to tell the world I am now a Christian. It matters not what cost I must pay, or what people say about me. I'm determined, I've made up my mind; I'll serve the Lord."

A young man who had been coming to a revival meeting was evidently under conviction. After the services one night the pastor went to him and said, "Son, why don't you turn your life over to Jesus?" He answered, "Well, my friends at school are not Christians, and I'm afraid they will laugh at me." The pastor said, "Why don't you turn your life over to Jesus and let God take care of it?"

The young man made a profession of faith and the next night at the service, the pastor went to him and asked, "How was your day?" He replied, "Oh, I had a good day. Nobody even suspected I was a Christian."

That's not it. That's not it at all. A Christian is one who stands up and claims, "I'm not ashamed. Jesus is mine!"

Years ago in England there lived a boy who didn't have a whole lot between his ears, and his friends called him a fool. He trusted Christ as his Savior, and he'd go around saying, "If I'm a fool, I'm a fool for Jesus." People started calling him "old fool for Jesus."

One day he was downtown and saw a man carrying one of those sandwich signs advertising for a restaurant. On each side it read "Eat at Joe's." The old boy had sense enough to get an idea from that.

He ran home and made him a sign. He painted it all up, put a sign on the front, a sign on the back, and walked down in the middle of town where all his friends were, and strutted down the street with a big smile on his face. As he approached his friends they read the sign on his front, "I'm a Fool for Jesus." And they said, "That poor old fool."

But you know, when a fellow like that goes by, you just feel compelled to read the back side, don't you? When they read the back side of the sign, it said "Whose Fool Are You?"

Friends, if I'm going to be a fool, I want to be God's fool. I don't want to be the devil's fool. I've seen some of the most brilliant minds in America that Satan has made an abject fool of, blown their minds, destroyed their personalities.

Accept the challenge! Don't be ashamed that you're a Christian!

I was in Rome a few years ago, and I visited that great coliseum, and I stood there and remembered the history I had read of that bloody acre, where pagans were hunting down Christians, not because they were wicked, but simply because they wouldn't deny their faith in Christ. They would bring them to that coliseum, thousands of people would gather (like we do for a football game), and they would take starved lions and turn them loose on the Christians. More than 50,000 Christians were killed in that

Roman coliseum. They suffered and they died. It was hard for those early Christians, but they accepted the challenge.

Polycarp, one of the early church fathers, was arrested and condemned to die. They tied him to the stake to burn him to death. When the executioner came to light the kindling at his feet, the governor said, "Halt! We don't want you to die, Polycarp. If you will recant your faith in Jesus, you can live."

Polycarp stretched himself against that stake, looked the governor straight in the eye, and said, "Eighty and six years have I followed Jesus, and not once has he forsaken me, and I'll not forsake him in this hour."

They ignited the flame and he went out into eternity because he had accepted the challenge.

I am going to ask you, my friend, would you become a Christian now? Will you make the choice? Would you choose Jesus Christ right now? Would you let God come in and change you? He will. He'll make out of you what you ought to be. He'll make out of you what you've never been able to make of yourself. God will do it for you.

Will you accept the challenge?

9

Three Besetting Sins of the Christian

Eddie Martin

As ye have therefore received Christ Jesus the Lord, so walk ye in him: rooted and built up in him, and stablished in the faith. COLOSSIANS 2:6-7

Let us not be desirous of vain glory, provoking one another, envying one another. GALATIANS 5:26

He that goeth forth and weepeth, bearing precious seed, shall doubtless come again with rejoicing, bringing his sheaves with him. PSALM 126:6

Many Christian leaders do not live in agreement with doctrinal statements and preaching. Many Christians leave undone the things that are Christian essentials. Many Christians do things that are against basic Christian principles. Now, I'm not talking about drunkenness or gambling. I know that you are not that kind of a person. But, this I know, many are guilty of respectable sins.

I. The Sin of Inconsistency

Many are guilty of the sin of inconsistency. In my life I have had to judge and confess over and over again the sin of inconsistency. I feel the text from Colossians is appropriate, for we need to be rooted and built up in him and established in the faith, and stop our inconsistent ways.

Our inconsistency reminds me of a fable. A beautiful princess was walking down a country lane, and a very handsome prince dressed in royal apparel come up to her, dropped on his knees and proposed marriage. Looking up into her eyes he said, "If only I could have thee, I would never want another. Will you give me your hand in marriage?"

She looked at the prince and replied, "Down the road about a mile my sister is following. She is far more beautiful than I. Go look at her, and if after having seen her you still desire me, I'll give you my answer."

The handsome prince got up and ran down the road. After a long time, he came running back, a look of great disappointment on his face. He said to the beautiful princess, "Why did you tell me that your sister was more beautiful than you? She is not to be compared with you in beauty."

The princess replied, "I know that, but didn't you say that if only you could have me you would never want another? If that is true, why did you even bother to go look at my sister?"

Isn't that true of most of us? We say, "Lord, thou are the fairest of ten thousand. All I need, Lord Jesus, I find in thee. I know I can't take money with me, and all the excitement of my life is nothing compared to my relationship to thee." No sooner is that devotion and love expressed than we go out following some other love and are unfaithful and inconsistent in our devotion to the lover of our soul, the Lord Jesus Christ.

1. We are guilty of inconsistency in our disposition.

A Christian should be the most joyful person on the face of God's earth. Christians should have sweet words and wholesome relationships with their loved ones and the people with whom they work. They should have a smile on their faces and a song in their hearts, and every word that comes over their lips should be one of praise, and joy, and rejoicing. Yet too many reserve their sweet words of commendation for people in a position to advance them and who can add to their gain. They use words of criticism and stinging, grouchy words for their families, those closest to them.

Grouchy persons are legion. The grouchy person and the grumbling person can be found everywhere. The growling person can be found in the Bible school. The growler can be found on the faculty. The grouchy, growler can be found in the family circle. The growler can be found in the pew, and the grouch can be found in the pulpit. The mother growls about the children when they don't pick up their clothing. The father growls when his supper is not prepared on time, or when the bills come due, and he complains that his wife is extravagant. The student growls about the food and about the way the school is being run. The church grouch growls about others, about the sermons, and about the preacher. The preacher growls about the people in the pews and the indifference in their hearts.

Ah, we've become a nation of grouches and growlers. Our dispositions are not sweet. We're inconsistent. It's a wonderful thing once in a while to come upon a man who is facing the problems of life with a smile on his face and victory in his soul. He makes no complaints, but he presses on until the victory's won.

Driving through the state of Ohio, I saw on a tombstone the name of a fellow by the name of "Gripe." I'd like to recommend that we enlarge Mr. Gripe's grave, and that we find all of the growlers, grouches, and gripers in the churches and in the homes, and that we put them in the grave and close it up. Then, place on the tombstone, "Here lie the grouchy growlers."

It's time for us to face this matter of our sour dispositions and call it sin. Don't talk to me about modernism. Don't talk to me about the movies. Don't talk to me about smoking teachers in the Sunday School. Let's talk about sour, grouchy dispositions. A grouchy, growling, sour disposition is as much sin in the sight of God as the things you label worldly.

Put your little spiritual umbrellas away. People come to my meetings, put up their little umbrellas and say, "Didn't he skin them tonight!" and everything falls on everybody else. Well, put your little umbrellas under the seat, because I have something to say to all of you.

2. We are inconsistent in our convictions.

It's wrong to desecrate our bodies with tobacco. It's wrong to gamble. It's wrong to commit adultery. It's wrong to spend Sunday afternoon glued to the tube. It's wrong, after being emotionally drained with the excitement of two games, to say to your family, "You go to church without me, I'm bushed." That's sin! Much being shown on television is immoral and unfit for family viewing. It's wrong to make athletic games our God. Pornography is wrong for a child of God. Making money our God is idolatry. Drinking alcohol in any form is wrong. Some Christians have let down the bars in the matter of their convictions. They have become worldly and lost their influence.

Some are inconsistent in preaching their convictions. Many preachers are preparing their sermons on top of the bread box. They're afraid that if they ring the changes on sin and point the finger to say, "Thou art the man," some liberal giver in the pew might get offended and no longer put his money into the church. We need to go to God in sackcloth and ashes, if anywhere along the line we've compromised in our convictions. Be a man of convictions, stand by them, live by them, and never compromise. Be consistent in your convictions.

3. We are inconsistent in the use of our spiritual gifts.

There are some people who could preach, but they don't. There are some people who can teach, but they don't. There are some people who can sing, but they don't. There are people who can visit, but they don't. There are some people who have wealth and talents for God, but they don't use them. You sing "Standing on the Promises," and I believe half the time you think it means "sitting on the premises."

Every Christian should use every gift for service that God has given him every hour of the day, of the week, of the month, and of the year until Jesus comes. If you're the type of Christian that runs in spurts, who gets all hepped up during the revival meeting and goes to church and serves God for about a month, and then falls by the wayside, you're guilty of inconsistency in the use of your gift.

4. We are inconsistent in our devotional lives.

Many Christians do not read their Bibles every day. Sometimes they read out of a sense of duty. We should read our Bibles every day to let God speak to our hearts.

If a person will spend fifteen minutes a day reading the Bible, he can read five pages a day in a Scofield Bible, and that's reading very slowly. If you spend fifteen minutes a day reading the Bible, you can read through the New Testament every sixty-seven days. You can read through the whole Bible every nine months. But you see, our problem is consistency. It's every day reading the Bible. It's every day getting alone with God in private prayer. It's every day having a family altar. We need consistency in talking to God in prayer, in reading the Bible, and in letting God talk to us.

Too many of us have a family altar that goes good for a month and then dies out. Too many of us read the Bible every other day or so. Too many of us allow "other things" to keep us away from our quiet time with God. A preacher is more than a maker of sermons; he's a maker of men. You can't make godly men until you, yourself are made into a man of God. You will do that only as you go to your knees, read your Bible, and get alone with God.

5. We are inconsistent in using our tongues.

Gossiping is terrible. A gossiper is as deadly as a child with a loaded revolver; as deadly as a drunken driver with a high-powered automobile. Gossiping has broken churches. Gossiping has robbed preachers' power. Gossiping has ruined the work of God in many places, and we preach against it. But, we sit down before deacons' meeting or at a church conference and have fried preacher. We criticize and gossip about preachers, other Christians, and the churches. That's all the conversation many people have.

God says that inconsistency with the tongue is wrong. It's wrong always to do idle talking. It's wrong for students to stand around talking about comic books when they ought to be talking about the Word of God. It's wrong to always be joking and laughing and engaging in frivolous talk. When I went to school, there were lots of fellows who never talked about anything that was sensible. Paul exhorts us to redeem the time, for the days are evil. There's no time to be wasted using our tongues in idle talk.

I bought a cheap fountain pen one time. It cost ninety-eight cents. I even received directions with that fountain pen, and the directions read like this: "When this pen begins to run too freely, it is a sign that it is almost empty." You get the point? Whenever a Christian is always talking nonsense, idle chatter, inconsistent with his tongue, put it down that he is almost empty.

Most of us will never be preachers or missionaries or great Christian heros, but I'll tell you one thing that can characterize the life of everyone of us. We can be a consistent, faithful, steadfast Christian. You can be, if you want to be. If you are, you will be rewarded at the judgment seat of Christ. It will be said, "Well done, thou good and faithful servant." It's not how many souls you've won to Christ, or how much money you've given, or how many people you have taught or visited. The thing that Jesus will reward will be faithfulness.

II. The Sin of Jealousy

Christians who are in places of responsibility, such as Sunday School teachers and leaders in the church, can be guilty of the sin of jealousy. If there is any sin that is committed by respectable, highly thought of Christians more than any other it is the sin of jealousy. The Bible says, "Let us not be desirous of vain glory, provoking one another, envying one another" (Gal. 5:26). The Bible says, "A sound heart is the life of the flesh: but envy the rottenness of the bones" (Prov. 14:30).

There are many, including this preacher, who have bowed their heads in shame and confessed that their hearts were filled with jealousy. There's possibly not a person in the Sunday morning service that has not been jealous of another teacher, another worker, or another Christian.

Jealousy gets great delight out of the failure of someone else. Jealousy is displeased with the success of someone else. The devil was jealous of God, and how it expressed itself in his old nature when he said, "I will ascend into heaven, I will exalt my throne above the stars of God: I will sit also upon the mount of the congregation . . . I will be like the most High" (Isa. 14:13-14). Jealousy, when it comes out in your life, is a definite expression of the old self nature and is evidence that your're not filled with the Holy Spirit.

Cain was jealous of his brother Abel, and what happened? He killed his brother in jealous hate. Jealousy is like that. If a man has a jealous heart, he begins to hate his brother in the Lord, and God says we should love one another. Joseph's brothers were jealous of him, and it divided the family. We need to be a united people, but when people are jealous of one another, it divides the body of Christ. You can't win victories for God divided.

Saul was jealous of David. The people began to sing that Saul had slain his thousands but David his tens of thousands. The first opportunity Saul had, he threw a javelin at David, trying to pin him against the wall. That's what jealousy will do. It will cause a man to try to kill one of his own soldiers. When no one else would go out to fight Goliath, David said, "God will deliver him into my hands," and he went out with a slingshot and a stone to deliver Israel. The boy who had fought his victories, Saul tried to pin to the wall with a javelin.

As Christian workers, how long is it going to take us to stop shooting down our own soldiers? How long is it going to take us to stop being jealous of some other Christian worker who is doing more than you're doing, winning more souls than you are winning, teaching a bigger class than you're teaching? How long is it going to take us to realize that we don't all have the same talents; that God has ordained and endowed some men with five talents and some with only one? How long is it going to take us to stop criticizing and condemning and talking about other leaders in the Lord's work, all because we're jealous that God didn't put us in their leadership position?

Miriam and Aaron were jealous of Moses, and what happened? Miriam was stricken with leprosy, and it stopped the camp of Israel for seven days. For seven days, while they waited for Miriam's recovery, they didn't march. The church is a marching church. The church is going through the wilderness now. I know of nothing that will stop the forward march of the church and hinder the Lord's work in our generation more than jealousy among God's people. It will stop the army. It will divide the camp. It will cause our wheels to stop rolling. It will cause the gospel trumpet to blast forth sour notes. It will paralyze the limbs that are carrying the gospel. We cannot afford to have one ounce of jealousy in our hearts.

If you are guilty of the sin of jealousy, how can you get rid of it? Admit it, confess it, and pray for the one about whom you are jealous.

F. B. Meyer, at one time, found that many of his church members were going over to hear G. Campbell Morgan, and Meyer became jealous. He said that the only way he got victory over his sin of jealousy was to confess it and to pray for Mr. Morgan. And, friend, the only way you are going to get victory over jealousy is to confess it and to start praying for the person about whom you are jealous. When you put the work of the Lord Jesus Christ ahead of your own selfish desire for glory and exaltation and advancement, there can be no jealousy in your heart when you see God blessing another's life and see souls being saved under the other man's ministry. You're not right with God if you can't rejoice with God's blessings on another Christian's life and witness.

You won't have any jealousy in your heart if you stop long enough to count your own blessings. I can't be jealous when I see what God has done for me and what God has given to me. I could never be jealous of Billy Graham, he's done so much for others. Every great building that's built, every great budget that's subscribed, every great victory won in the church is going to bless and help you and your church.

If you've got a jealous streak in your soul, count your own blessings, and see what God's done for you. You can't have jealousy remain in your life very long.

III. The Sin of a Compassionless Heart for Souls

Respectable Christians are guilty of the sin of a compassionless heart for souls. How long has it been since you've left your home and knocked on the door in the neighborhood to talk to a man about his soul? How long has it been since you talked to someone on the job about his soul? How long has it been since you wept for a lost soul?

The sin of a compassionless heart is evidenced in cold, drab services and in sterile, dry Bible teaching. Often we do not teach or preach to reach the lost, and many times we don't give an invitation for sinners to receive Christ. It's been months in many churches since a sinner came to the altar to get right with God. Many of you have people in your church who don't know how to lead a soul to Christ. Why? I'll tell you why. There's no soul-winning fire in the pulpit or in the pew.

There's only one way we can take America for Christ. We're not going to do it with the evangelistic ministry of one man or a group of evangelists. An evangelist may hold an overwhelmingly successful city-wide or country-wide evangelistic crusade; however, in one year there will have been more children born in that area than there were souls born again in that crusade. We're losing ground!

How are we going to take the world for Jesus Christ? We must get back to the way God ordained. Every Christian, every layman, every student, every preacher, every teacher, must gear his life to win souls to Jesus Christ.

D. L. Moody made it the practice of his life to witness to somebody every day. When I read that as a student, I put on my overcoat, filled my pockets with tracts and for three years I walked the streets of Chicago. I went in bars night after night, talking to people about their souls. Don't tell me that they can't be won for Christ. I remember the man that I led to Jesus Christ at 812 North Clark Street the first week I was in Moody Bible Institute. He was one of the worst drunkards, one of the worst reprobates who ever walked the streets of Chicago. Today he's a well-repected gentleman. There are lost souls within a stone's throw of every place you'll put your foot in your city. The greatest sin you can commit as a respectable Christian is to go week after week and not try to win a soul to the Lord Jesus Christ.

Some men have gone through human hell to win souls. William Carey got a map and put down the need of every country. With the Great Commission burning in his soul, Carey said, "O God, do you want to use me?" And God said, "I want you to go." Carey went to India. For seven years he and Mr. Thomas, his helper, labored without winning a convert. After seven years, they led a man to Jesus Christ who was willing to be baptized publicly. Seven long years Carey preached and witnessed before he won one soul to Jesus Christ.

John Wesley used to ride on horseback over five thousand miles a year to win souls.

When the doctor warned George Whitefield, "Whitefield, you've got to slow down. You can preach only four hours a day and six hours on Sunday," Whitefield rose from his sick bed and said, "Doctor, do you want me to rust out for God?"

David Brainerd dragged his consumptive body into the woods of the upper forks of the Delaware and for five years, night and day, he prayed and fasted and preached. He loved and prayed and led those Indians to Jesus Christ. After five years, he came staggering out of the woods to die in Jerusha Edwards' arms. He loved her, but Brainerd loved souls more than he loved Jerusha Edwards. Three months after he died in her arms, she died too.

I see the vision of Livingstone going into the heart of Africa. He had heard Robert Moffat say, "I have often stood and watched the smoke rise from a thousand villages where no missionary has every been." That graphic statement so broke Livingstone's heart that he said, "I'll go to those thousand villages, and I'll go to ten thousand more with the help of God, and carry the gospel of Jesus Christ." He cut his way into the heart of Africa. See him battling the bush, the heat, the swarms of mosquitoes which came to eat on his flesh, and the thirty-one attacks of fever which struck him down.

Men like these have gone through human hell to win souls to Christ, and many Christians today won't walk across the street to talk to a lost person. We've got elevators and planes and trains and cars and every advantage to reach souls for Christ, but our hearts have grown cold. We've lost our love for lost souls. We're committing the sin of compassionless hearts toward the lost.

One day I sat in Torrey-Gray Auditorium at Moody Bible Institute and thrilled with the testimonies of victories for God. My mind drifted back to the day when Edward Kimball, a businessman, walked into a shoe store in Boston to talk to D. L. Moody, his Sunday School pupil. He found the 135 pound, seventeen-year-old boy wrapping shoes. Kimball said, "I put my trembling hand on Moody's shoulder, and I told him about the love of God. I made a miserable failure." But for years, Mr. Moody could feel the throb of that warm hand. Moody lifted his heart to God right there by the shoe racks and asked Jesus to save him. Because a layman went out to tell a lost boy about the love of Christ, Moody was saved and his witness and influence spread around the world. A layman, doing personal witnessing, led one boy to Jesus Christ. That's the most successful program I know of to take a town, a world for Christ.

Will you, as a Christian, go everywhere asking people what they think about the Lord Jesus Christ? You pastors, you laymen, you young people go back into your lives and your homes and into your churches set on fire for God! What a tragedy if your hearts have grown cold for souls.

Respectable Christians, and yet we are guilty of the sin of inconsistency, the sin of jealousy, the sin of a compassionless heart toward the lost souls of men! May God forgive us and cleanse our hearts anew for his service.

Contributors

Jack R. Taylor is a native of Texas. He is a graduate of Hardin-Simmons University and Southwestern Baptist Theological Seminary. For seventeen years, he was pastor of the Castle Hills First Baptist Church in San Antonio before becoming president of Dimensions in Christian Living, an international ministry. He is the author of seven Broadman books.

James Robison is a native of Texas. He attended San Jacinto Junior College and East Texas Baptist College. He became a Christian at age fifteen and began his evangelistic ministry at age eighteen. He is involved in crusade evangelism and has a television ministry.

Jack Stanton is a native of Illinois and is the professor of evangelism at Redford School of Theology and the director of the Institute of Evangelism at Southwest Baptist College, Bolivar, Missouri. He is the former director of evangelism for the Colorado Baptist General Convention and the Kansas-Nebraska Convention of Southern Baptists. For fourteen years, he served as director of personal and mass evangelism with the Home Mission Board, SBC. He was co-author of the *Southern Baptist Handbook of Evangelism* and numerous articles, papers, and booklets on evangelism.

Mike Gilchrist is a native of Louisiana. The first three years of his ministry was spent as a youth evangelist in the South, followed by five years in the pastorate. Since that time, he has been involved in nationwide and international evangelism in more than 700 crusades.

Sam T. Cathey is a native of Arkansas and a graduate of Ouachita Baptist University. He is a past president of the Southern Baptist Evangelists Conference and has served as a pastor in Arkansas and Michigan for over ten years. He is the author of two books and numerous articles, papers, and booklets on evangelism.

Angel Martinez is a native of Texas. He is a graduate of Baylor University and Southern Baptist Theological Seminary. He is the author of nine books, and has completed the task of memorizing the entire New Testament.

Jim Wilson is a native of Alabama. He is a graduate of Wheaton College and Southern Baptist Theological Seminary. He has spoken to numerous youth and adults in conferences, seminars, crusades and revivals. Among his honors has been a listing in *Outstanding Young Men of America.* His father, T. W. Wilson, is associate to Billy Graham.

Bill C. Penley is a native of North Carolina and a graduate of Tennessee Temple College, Temple Baptist Theological Seminary, and has attended Southeastern Baptist Theological Seminary. Before beginning a ministry in evangelism in 1969, he pastored churches in Tennessee, Alabama, and North Carolina, for seventeen years. He is the immediate past president of the Southern Baptist Evangelists Conference.

Eddie Martin was the president of the Southern Baptist Evangelists Conference for 1978-79. A native of Pennsylvania, he is a graduate of Moody Bible Institute and has been a Southern Baptist evangelist for over thirty years. He is the author and editor of the *Law of the Harvest,* a witness training program. He is a member of the First Baptist Church, Jacksonville, Florida.